Heretics' Faith

Also by Fredric John Muir:

A Reason for Hope: Liberation Theology Confronts a Liberal Church

Maglipay Universalist: The Unitarian Universalist Church of the Philippines

Essays by the author found in:

Redeeming Time: Endowing Your Church with the Power of Covenant

With Purpose and Principle: Essays about the Seven Principles of Unitarian Universalism

Creating Safe Congregations: Toward an Ethic of Right Relations

Heretics' Faith

Vocabulary for Religious Liberals

Fredric John Muir

Heretics' Faith: Vocabulary for Religious Liberals
©2001 by Fredric John Muir

Library of Congress Card Number: 2001116224
ISBN 0-9707903-0-9

Cover artwork by William Heuer.

Acknowledgment and Dedication

This book is dedicated to the Unitarian Universalist Church of Annapolis, an outstanding congregation. Their love and support of me, and my ministry, has been more than any minister could ask for.

Contents

An Introduction

It's not easy being a Unitarian Universalist.

Just a cursory look at our history clearly shows that this isn't a recent development. Whether it's our history in North America or that of the free-thinking church reforms of the third century of the Common Era—perhaps the context has changed, the issues are different, the names and places vary—but since its beginnings Unitarians and Universalists have been understood as out of the mainstream and on the fringe. We have always been thought of as a heretical faith.

The world *heresy* comes from the Greek *hairesis* and means 'choice': as a heretic, you choose. There are all kinds of heresies, but being a religious heretic has always meant not going along with official religious doctrines and creeds. Unitarian Universalism's particular heresy is that we are religious liberals.

Being a liberal is currently not popular—the word alone strikes fear or animosity in the hearts of many. But like *heretic, liberal* has a special meaning for Unitarian Universalists: its root means 'to be generous and open.' As religious liberals, we seek deeper and wider understanding, greater tolerance, broader definition, more inclusive language; we want to stretch our minds and souls, pushing the limits of thought and spirit, redefining the boundaries of tradition and orthodoxy. And so, as religious liberals we have committed heresy and appear out of the mainstream, standing at the fringe.

Yet we are at the fringe not only by heretical and liberal thought, but by word, by vocabulary. We have isolated ourselves by speaking a language that very few understand and appreciate—including some of our own members! We have chosen a vocabulary of faith that few recognize or comprehend. In the process of shaping our liberal and heretical faith, the vocabulary we have chosen is so far from the traditional spiritual, theological, and religious mainstream that enunciating our beliefs for others has posed a significant if not insurmountable challenge.

What has added to the difficulty and confusion is that religious fundamentalists, and now the religious right, co-oped the religious dictionary by cutting out all the words they wanted, assigning their definitions to these words, and then pasting them into a new dictionary and calling it the official one. And if that wasn't amazing enough, religious liberals went them one better: we didn't say a thing about it. In fact we were so caught up in the splendors of science, rationalism, humanism, and the demystification of sacred scripture that we practically helped them: that was language, those were words, we told ourselves and others, for which we simply had no more use.

We have limited and handicapped ourselves by giving away this dictionary. Those are the words of religion. Just as every facet of life has its own vocabulary, so does faith. And while humanism is valuable and has a place, often this language does not work. It has been said that religion and spirituality are poetry and song. In this sense, the scientific and rational language of humanism doesn't always fit, doesn't go far enough, isn't flexible. Those like Joseph Campbell, Starhawk, Matthew Fox, Alice Walker, and Margot Adler and their books and lectures on spirituality, neopaganism, mythology, and mysticism have gone a long way in helping us understand the metaphoric and symbolic value of religious story and language.

When we don't use the language of faith, people outside our small circle of liberal religious friendships have no idea what we're talking about. I'm reminded of a class in preaching (homiletics) I took during my doctoral studies. One of the assigned books was a protestant lectionary which detailed all the Bible readings for each Sunday of the year—it even included suggested sermon themes, liturgical garb and colors, rituals, prayers, responses, and so on. For me it was like reading a script in a foreign language. There were words and concepts in that book I had ever heard. When my professor announced that not only would we use the lectionary as a reference tool, but the two times we preached to the class we were to base our one-hour service on the lectionary, I panicked. What was I going to do? I called my professor. Certainly, I told myself, he can't expect me, a Unitarian Universalist, a non-Christian, to follow the protestant lectionary. I explained my circumstance and concern. He listened. I told him it was like being in a foreign land and not knowing the language. Then, after I essentially pleaded for his understanding, he uttered his only words to me, words that still reverberate in my mind. He said: "Mr. Muir, I suggest that it's time you learn the language. See you in class."

I know I wouldn't have come to this realization on my own. Similarly, I don't think we've come to understand the importance and value of faith language by ourselves. It has taken the religious right pounding away at us, defining and using words like *sin, atonement,* and *evil; salvation, prayer,* and *blessing; grace, scripture,* and *God*—words that still have value, meaning, and heritage in our tradition and in our lives—it has taken religious orthodoxy and fundamentalism to get us to notice that we have been coming up short-handed.

If we hope to spread our liberal religious gospel, we must become familiar and comfortable with the vocabulary of faith. We must learn the language! As Unitarian Universalists, we bring a liberal and heretical spirit to this vocabulary that can breathe new life into ancient words. May this book make a contribution to that endeavor.

Angels

Peter Fleck writes: "Angels, from the Greek *angelos* meaning *messenger*, according to the dictionary, are messengers of God, carriers of God's messages, especially addressed to human beings." While the value of and fascination with these other-worldly carriers of divine tidings are spiritually intriguing and personally fulfilling as well as commercially profitable, the historical role that angels play in the life of the religious has been overlooked if not forgotten. As if a testimonial to the groundswell of their popularity, a *Newsweek* cover story reported: "To the ancient Israelites, angels were proud members of God's heavenly court, fierce captains of a heavenly army who defended nations, delivered powerful messages, and spent their time singing God's praises." Found in Judaism as well as Christianity and Islam, angels are not a simple monolithic, homogeneous lot; there is a celestial hierarchy, with divisions according to role, power, proximity to the Almighty, and more. It isn't a position that brings with it equal opportunity, affirmative action, or much room for advancement. It is tough work, for a tough boss, with lots of tough love!

There are several messages—whether heavenly sent or not I don't know—that an interest in angles puts forth. Let's begin with a story:

An ancient legend has it that when God was creating the world, four angels approached the Almighty. The first one asked, "How are you doing it?" The second, "Why are you doing it?" The third, "Can I be of help?" The fourth,

"What's it worth?" The first was a scientist; the second, a philosopher; the third, an altruist; and the fourth, a real estate agent. A fifth angel watched in wonder and applauded in sheer delight. This one was the mystic.

If "life is alive" as Howard Thurman declared, then the Cosmos is teeming with possibility, with potential—it vibrates, it rushes and gushes, the Cosmos is perpetually and inexhaustibly present with secrets beyond the imaginings of one's craziest dreams. So why not angels? The story would lead us to answer, Because most haven't been nurtured in the ways of the mystic. Our education has been from the academy, where the questions are how, why, and what. These questions are important and have produced many wonders. But part of the fallout of an overdeveloped left brain, of too many academic questions and not enough mystical nurturing, has been no longer seeing, knowing, and feeling that "life is alive."

Given this state of mind and education, it is little wonder that the existence of angels is thought to be a highly unlikely possibility—which is, of course, a very rational, logical, left-brain type of conclusion. It's not something many spend a lot of time thinking about. But what if the language is changed? Call them messages from God, grace, secrets of the Cosmos, synchronicity, luck—these have an appealing ring to them, intriguing, even likely. All of these imply an openness to life, creating the opportunity for something to happen. A lot can be said for being aware and open to the opportunities, good fortune, and pleasure which exists around us, though it's very easy and quite often more comfortable to close down rather than open up. It was Ramakrishna who said, "The winds of god's grace are always blowing and we only have to raise our sails."

To say these winds are brought by angels, angels sent by the divine, may be going too far. Yet we are of the Cosmos, which embodies everything, a Cosmos that is alive. The winds of the Cosmos are in and about us, always. Some of what we hear and feel and know has an angel-like (angelic) quality to it. It can seem miraculous. Willa Cather said it this way: "Miracles seem to me to rest not so much upon our faces or voices or healing power coming suddenly from far off but upon our perception being made finer, so that for a moment our eyes can see and our ears can hear what is about us always."

Often some don't allow these messages of grace or help or encouragement to come through because they've blocked themselves off, either by cutting themselves off from others or by limiting their perception of the world or by refusing to take needed risks. How easy it is to shut down all one's senses, convinced that we know what to expect, similar to "a man who had been lost in the desert. Later, when describing his ordeal to his friends, he told how, in sheer despair, he had knelt down and cried out to God for help. 'And did God answer your prayer?' he was asked. 'Oh no! Before that could happen an explorer appeared and showed me the way.'" Perhaps there's more that goes on around us and happens to us than we know, understand, or even recognize. It's not that we can't see it, it's that we don't know how to see it. We have to change our glasses, get some new lenses, change our focus.

The fascination with angels may be simply an attempt to come to grips with things we don't understand. We each have our own way of explaining the messages that arrive at our feet—unasked for, undeserved, sometimes unwanted. I don't believe in angels, but I believe in the angelic; I don't believe in messengers from heaven on high, but I believe in the messages I receive, messages of insight, centering, love, and prompting; I don't believe in heavenly beings who march in hierarchical legions or who have been assigned my case until removed, but I do believe in the neighbor or friend, stranger or acquaintance who seemingly out of nowhere makes an unexpected delivery. And I like to think that it's because my sails are raised, my ears can hear, and my eyes can see. I even know that sometimes it's the same wind from another time, the same sight I've seen or sounds I've heard dozens of times before, but this time, this time it was different. Why? I think it was angelic. Why not?

Armageddon

History is littered with visions and predictions of the Last Days. Many of us are familiar with the most famous of the predictors, the early Christians, who encountered what all end-of-the-world-as-we-know-it groups must eventually confront: when it doesn't happen, they had to quickly retrace their steps and, before too many stray, come up with another meaningful and convincing explanation as to why the miscalculation occurred as well as why dubious or disillusioned followers should bother believing again. In the Christian Scriptures, Paul predicts the coming of the Final Days; it's in the words of Jesus Christ, he tells his readers. As time goes on, he has to keep revising his message because it becomes clear that everyday life as he knows it is going to go on.

But if it had come to an end, if events had transpired as the early Christians had supposed, it all would have come down to Armageddon, which, according to Revelation 16:16, is the location for the final battle between the forces of good and evil. It is at Armageddon where this is going to happen. I use "Armageddon" in a more general sense, simply to refer to the destructive ending of the world.

I have never been one to pay much attention to whether or not I've aligned myself with the forces of the good and righteous so as to have salvation, so as to be among those who are called back after the battle, to be among "the 144,000 who have been redeemed from the earth" (Revelation 14:3). As I read through the apocalyptic visions of Revelation and its predecessor, Daniel, I figure that it's anybody's guess as to what they mean. This is precisely what has happened: many have tried to give these visions their own interpretation, often accompanied by personal, first-hand messages from God, a sure way to lend authenticity to their version.

Twentieth-century realities like nuclear war, pro-Zionist politics, and Cold War antagonisms have all fueled end-of-the-world scenarios, including best-selling books like Hall Lindsay's *The Late Great Planet Earth* and its sequel *The 1980s, Countdown to Armageddon,* and John Walvoor's best-selling *Armageddon, Oil and the Middle East Crisis.*

But all of this is quite new to me. I was raised in a home and a church where very little mention was made of Daniel and Revelation or of the ending of the world. I was urged to do the right thing not because I would then be part of the 144,000, among the saved, but simply because doing the right thing had value in and of itself. You did it because, well, because it was the right thing to do! This is what being a good Christian meant to me, this is what I was told. It wasn't until later that someone told me about Judgment Day, about the Rapture, about Armageddon. And I then had a difficult time figuring out how to reconcile this with the Christian scripture's image I'd been brought up with of a God (and son) who were omnipotently loving, caring, nurturing, forgiving, and supporting. Needless to say, it didn't make much sense to me, so I just forgot about it. I could easily forget about it because in my suburban Chicago, middle-class—which is to say comfortable—environment, an apocalyptic story was not very important. But stories of the world's destruction have been important to many.

Many of the early world-destruction stories are ancient, often pagan, dating far back into time before the first millennium. They were part of an understanding reached through simple, repetitive observation of the way nature worked. Ancient civilizations lived and died by the land, a relationship that was far more basic and elemental than anything we can begin to comprehend. Rosemary Radford Ruether notes in *Gaia & God* that most of these stories are "versions of [the] basic myth of the death of nature through yearly drought."

But this wasn't good enough for some. The early Hebrew community, for example, was trying to establish itself as a legitimate religion. They had to convince those around them that their God was better, i.e., more powerful than the pantheon of already established gods with which they were competing. In fact, early Hebrew religious history, theology, and belief were in many ways simply a matter of that community going their religious neighbors one better.

So, they took the creation/destruction stories and made them their own by revision. Ruether explains: "In their hands the stories are moralized and placed in the context of the historical fortunes of Israel. World destruction, through floods, drought, and trampling armies, becomes punishment by God, retribution for failure to obey the laws of the one God, who controls nature and history from above."

The leap from Jewish to Christian apocalypticism is neatly bridged in the simple fact that both Jesus and Paul were deeply rooted in the Jewish stories of world destruction. Jesus suggested and Paul insisted that the end was near. While both were wrong, and Paul especially had to revise his message considerably, the story remained the same: the world is coming to an end—repent, be saved, and have eternal life.

It seems to have fallen to secularists and religious liberals to dismiss and make light of the apocalyptic visions as found in the Bible and heard from television and radio preachers as well as read among current Armageddon-pronouncing writers. But while the messages of fanaticism have been rejected by many, what has taken their place? Political anarchy and environmental disaster seem to top the current list of apocalyptic events, and nuclear war remains a threat. But what is different about these secularized editions of Armageddon, and what clearly sets them off from the religious, is that they appear to be final. That is, after the destruction there is no rebirth, no saved, no remnant to carry on; there's no hope—or if there is, the authors aren't talking about it. Perhaps this was part of the difficulty many had with religious apocalypticism: in a perverted and ironic kind of way, it was too rosy for the reality-based twenty-first century folks. It's almost as if they are saying: If the world is going to end, everyone's got to go; there will be no prisoners and no survivors.

Even though I didn't grow up with the apocalyptic message, either religious or secular, and it wasn't really until high school that some semblance of fear regarding the world's ending even entered my mind, today's children are growing up with a very different awareness. Whether they want it or not, today it's very difficult for any child or youth to avoid the secular message that all's not right with the world. It's not a difficult leap from that to, "Is the world coming to an end?" and the question I have heard from some, "Will I make it to adulthood?"

Perhaps the apocalyptic question of whether or not the world is coming to an end is the wrong question. You see, we are of the universe, the Cosmos, and like the origins of the destruction myths—the apocalyptic stories of this universe—there is a process to nature, there is a giving and taking, a birthing and dying, a coming and going. This is the nature of the world, of all of life—this is the one great law that cannot be refuted: the Cosmos is always changing, and yet is always in balance. The question, then, is this: In my small corner of the Cosmos, what am I doing to live in harmony with this law, and is the manner in which I live destructive to the balance of all living things on earth? In other words, am I living my life, am I related with others, in a way that will maintain the integrity, or sacredness, of the universe and all that is in it?

The universe is my home, my place of being. I belong here. I don't know what the future holds, whether or not there is an afterlife, an Armageddon—maybe just space and silence. But I do know what Tony Hoagland captures in a poem he calls "A Change of Plans":

It's tiring, this endless revision / of our ideas of a world / which is being continually revised—/. . . . What we've learned is mostly / not to be so smart—to believe. / Remember how the reptiles after generations of desire / to taste the yellow flowers, thrust our wings one day and lifted / from the ground? / Being birds by that time / their appetites had changed. / But they kept flying. (*Sweet Ruin*)

Apocalyptic predictions come and go, and explanations for why we are here are many—as Hoagland writes, the revised plans are many. But this we all know: we are here, right now. This we can hold on to, and there is no going back; like the birds whose appetites had changed, we too have to keep flying. And in this flight, there is always hope. Just as seasons change and these cycles in which we live replenish and refresh our earth home, we can take heart in knowing that we each have an opportunity, every day, to contribute to the well-being and balance and joy of life on earth.

Authority

By whose authority are we church? By whose authority do we act in the name of our church? By whose authority do we sponsor, ordain, and call ministers? By whose authority do I officiate at weddings and unions, christenings and dedications, funerals and memorials? By whose authority do I pray at the bedside of a dying patient, write a sermon, dedicate a building, visit a member, counsel a family, ask a person to leave the congregation? By whose authority do we ask for a pledge of money, a commitment of time, and a show of support for each other? As is asked of Jesus, I am asking myself, and I am asking you too: "Who is it that gave you this authority?"(Luke 20:2)

Most of us have at some time in our lives been associated with congregations that had a variety of answers to this authority issue. But I would suggest that there was always a central one, one around which all the other answers revolved. And while other responses were important, at the core of any faith is a single, dominating, revered source of authority which all the others follow, from which all the others originate.

In Judaism, that single source of authority is captured perfectly in the musical *Fiddler on the Roof.* In the prologue, Tevye tells the audience: "You may ask, how did these traditions get started? I'll tell you: I don't know. But it's tradition! And because of our traditions, everyone knows who he is and what God expects him to do."

Tradition! Tradition tells the Jew everything. "Why do we do it this way or that? Because that's the way it's always been done!" You don't question tradition.

In Roman Catholicism, the source of authority is the hierarchy. When in doubt, ask a church official. And when a church official doesn't know, he asks a higher church official, and on up. The hierarchy decides and rules, which I'm convinced is one of the reasons American Catholics always appear to give the world Catholic church hierarchy so much trouble: it's very difficult to blend Roman Catholic theocracy with government by the people.

In my second year of seminary I was taking a class in American church history. We weren't too far along in the semester—maybe just a couple of weeks—when in one of the lectures the professor stopped and asked a classmate if he needed help. I turned to see a fellow student, about my age (24), sobbing. Class stopped for a moment while he got a drink. When he came back he apologized for the disruption and explained that he'd been raised in a Roman Catholic home and had attended Roman Catholic schools. Coming to this seminary was the first non-Catholic context in which he'd ever found himself. And he was shocked, stunned, and overwhelmed with what he was learning about the Catholic Church and the rest of religious America. It seems he'd never heard anything but the Catholic Church hierarchical line and now he was making up for lost time.

This is extreme, I know, but it does happen. In the Roman Church, the hierarchy is the source of authority: what it says is law. Yes, there are brilliant, compassionate, justice-seeking Catholic laypeople and officials. But when push comes to shove, the final source of church authority rests within the hierarchy: nuns, priests, bishops, cardinals, and Pope.

In Protestantism, some denominations are more steeped in tradition than others; some churches have very elaborate hierarchies while others have virtually none. But for the Protestant church, the final source of authority is the Gospels. It's the Gospels that tell the story of Jesus Christ; it's the Gospels that provide the church with the teachings for its believers. The Gospels are the source of Jesus' message, and nowhere in that message does it say anything about the ultimacy of either tradition or hierarchy.

Tradition, hierarchy, and the Gospels—these three, then, are a trinity of authority in those religious groups with which we are most familiar. And it's not that we as Unitarian Universalists reject these. Certainly we have our traditions, we even have a hierarchy, and the New Testament Gospels have always been a source of authority for many. But the final source of authority for most Unitarian Universalists is their own experience. Experience is the focusing lens through which life is viewed, through which all other possible authority is seen. A meditation from Clinton Lee Scott puts into words the way many believe:

> People have long dreamed of the time proclaimed by prophets, of ultimate fulfillment. The dream remains, but it is sobered by human responsibility. Once it was supposed that an unseen guiding hand rested upon our shoulder, and that a plan not of our making guaranteed high destiny for us. Now we are learning (ever so slowly) that we have no infallible guide. We must take our chances with the changing fortunes of life. Only we can underwrite the lofty expectations. In the quest for fullness we have the heritage of history, intelligence, and goodwill. That is all we have, and this is all we need. (*Promise of Spring*)

Not by tradition, hierarchy, nor prophetic teaching alone do we make our decisions. Our living, our religious life, the life that is shared in a congregation will be influenced by all three of these (and probably more). But the final source of authority will be our own understanding, our own feelings, what we believe is best; it will rest on our own experience—what Scott calls "the heritage of history, intelligence, and goodwill."

This must be our test too. Just how firmly rooted are we in our authority, in our own experience? How deep is our faith? The authority by which we do these things is rooted in an answer that is sustained by an uncompromising commitment to do what is just, what is fair and compassionate, what our "history, intelligence, and goodwill" demand that we must do. This is our faith. Taken together, this is the faith I preach, it is the faith that we have come to rely on, it is the faith that keeps our coming in and going out, it is the faith that gives us the authority that we must have to respond to the chief priests and scribes of our day. An uncompromising commitment to do what is just, what is fair and compassionate, what our "history, intelligence, and goodwill" demand that we must do. This faith to do what is right, this faith is rooted in several ongoing, powerful sources of authority.

The first is passion. If there was a single word that had to describe the Unitarian Universalist faith, it would be *passionate*. Our religious pilgrimage or odyssey begins in passion. "Religion, in [this] sense, is like baseball or any other form of play or art." In his book, *At Home in Creativity,* Bruce Southworth quotes Henry Wieman:

> The professionals who play in the big leagues render a great service to baseball. Baseball would certainly not pervade our national life as it does if it were not for these big leagues. But if you want to find out the true spirit of baseball in all the glory of a passion, you must not go to the big leagues. You must go to the backyard, the sandlot, the side street, and the school ground. There it is not a profession, it is a passion. When a passion becomes a profession, it often ceases to be a passion. That is as true of religion as it is of baseball. Among the professionals you find a superb mastery and a great technique, but not too frequently the pure devotion. Perhaps in baseball the passion is not too important, but in religion it is all important. A religion that is not passionate simply is not worth considering. Therefore, I say, we need more sandlot religion. The professional, whether [Oriole] or Methodist, controls inordinately our baseball and our religion.

Unitarian Universalism is very much of a "sandlot religion," very grass-roots in the sense that belief and faith are close to the believer: without a reliance on tradition, hierarchy, or dogma the door is wide open for unencumbered passion. In Unitarian Universalism, our passion for faith, our passion for religion, our passion to do what is right is the authority by which we are church, the authority by which we do these things. We are a people of passion who keep close to our heart the stirrings of spirit.

Another source of authority for us is the congregation itself. Believing that there is fairness, compassion, justice, and insight in collective wisdom and self-direction, we practice congregational polity. This means that the members of a church are the final source of authority in all institutional matters: ordaining and calling ministers as well as firing them; determining what is taught to our children and adults as well as who will teach it. As the source of authority, power is not invested in one or two individuals, but rests in the group.

This is not an easy way to run the church. Yet I couldn't imagine anything better—I wouldn't trade it for anything different. I trust our collective wisdom, I honor what the congregation says, I believe that there is a spirit of integrity, honesty, and sincerity in the congregational insight and wisdom that bends toward what is right. In this authority we put great confidence and trust, though it is sometimes tempting to lean another way.

The authority that is rooted in passion, the authority rooted in collective, congregational wisdom, these simply won't have the same meaning, power, or significance unless accompanied by the authority rooted in deliberate, intentional, heartfelt caring and companionship. The support we give to each other, the attention given the stranger—we must never take these for granted.

We are all in this together, in the life of the church, in day-to-day life and struggle. We must lead with our hearts, and where our hearts go our passion and wisdom will follow. We are a caring community. If we are not prepared to respond in a caring, heart-filled manner, then it's time to close the doors and move elsewhere. An authority firmly rooted in the heart is an authority rooted in power. It is an authority that will see and help others to see a vision that might appear as unclear.

There is a story about two travelers on their way to Japan. They were standing at the rail of the ship looking out upon the vast open sea. After but a few moments, one of the men turned about and walked away, disappointment written on his countenance. Throughout the day, the man returned to the deck rail and then turned his back upon the scene, each time appearing more disconsolate than before.

Finally the second traveler, who had remained at the rail, felt compelled to ask this fellow traveler what it was that made him so downcast on what was supposedly a pleasure trip. The first man replied that he had been told that at this point of the voyage he would be able to see Mount Fuji rising in the distance. However, the haze over the water was apparently not going to lift, depriving him of a sight that he had so long anticipated.

Taking him by the arm, his shipmate led the man back to the rail of the ship and said quietly, "Look higher." The traveler, raising his eyes above the haze, saw, in all its beauty and majesty, the great mountain peak.

Who has not felt disappointment at being unable to catch an unencumbered view of the picture we long to see? Who has not needed to be taken by the arm and given support? Who has not received the companionship we needed? Who doesn't know the feelings of rejection, isolation, confusion, and disappointment? We all know how it feels and what it is like. Let us not refuse direction from the heart, for in reaching out to each other is the power and authority of love and truth and grace.

We are members and friends of a faith tradition called Unitarian Universalism. As such, like anyone else in any other faith community, we too must respond to the questions: "Tell us, by what authority are you doing these things? Who is it who gave you this authority?" The answer rests in religious passion, collective wisdom, and the strength of heartfelt outreach. With these three we will answer the high priests and scribes of today; these are all the authority we need; these must be the essence and building blocks of our faith.

Beginning

I've read hundreds of times that Americans have a love affair with the automobile. If that is our nation's first-love of choice, then close on its heels would have to be something far less tangible, but equally as liberating: our love of beginnings. Though my list is not very complete (which means I left a lot of room for you to finish it), here are just a few of the more pithy ways we've canonized this near-religious faith in beginnings: "Live each day as if it were the first day of the rest of your life." "If at first you don't succeed, try, try again." "A journey of a thousand miles begins with but a single step." "It's never too late to have a happy childhood." How well we know them all! The notion of "starting over" has littered the national consciousness and language to the point of saturation—everybody can do it, in myriad ways: a new job, a change of cities or homes or spouses or lovers, a new child, a vacation, a new hairdo, a weight loss and new wardrobe—how about cosmetic surgery?

Yes, we have a love affair with starting over. But there is no such thing as a beginning—at least not for us, not in the way I will speak about. Let's start in a place no less well-respected than the Bible, in the wisdom of Ecclesiastes (1:5, 9), where it tells us: "The sun rises and the sun goes down, / and hurries to the place where it rises . . . / What has been is what will be, / and what has been done is what will be done; / there is nothing new under the sun."

And so it goes, and goes and goes. There aren't really beginnings, points for starting over. Life is on a continuum, and the best we can get are continuations where the edges of new experiences are always shaded with their predecessors—kind of a spillage from one experience to the next. It's not very sexy-sounding, but perhaps is more accurate.

There will be those who will argue that their life has been shaped by beginnings and endings. But most will agree, however hesitatingly and begrudgingly, that life is simply a continuation. I must admit that I am torn between the two. I like the idea of a periodic fresh start, a clean slate, living today as if it were the first day of the rest of my life and all that that means. Yet I know for certain that with every so-called fresh start I make, I carry with me a trunkload of psychological and spiritual hand-me-downs that make the image of "A New Me" ridiculous and far from exact.

Why the need for starting over? What is it about "beginning" that holds such an attraction? Why is the message of Ecclesiastes such a difficult one to hear? I can think of several interrelated reasons. One is control, control of living—which is really the need to control death, as in to postpone or even avoid it (imagine avoiding death!). I mean, the fundamentalists don't have the corner on the denial of death—religious liberals can play that game too, anybody can. As long as you can start over, and you name the terms, rebirthing yourself forever, just think how long you can hold off death. If you can just keep changing jobs, remarrying, building a new home, finding Jesus or God or karma, just think of all the beginnings.

Then there's boredom, as in Ecclesiastes: "What has gone on is what shall go on, / And there is nothing new under the sun." Boredom, which for some is nothing more than a small, daily kind of death, is to be prevented at all costs. What better way to deal with boredom than to start over, to begin afresh, the take the first step in the journey of a thousand miles?

And of course, there's frustration and dissatisfaction—if you don't succeed, keep trying. Why? Because you want to get it right: "Before I die, I'm going to do this the right way!" As if to suggest to the gods above, "When I'm satisfied, then you can take me"—which of course makes no sense at all! Ah, to start over, to make a new beginning, and this time, to get it right—no mistakes, no problems.

It's probably impossible to live with a sense of freshness, of beginning all the time. Thorton Wilder put it this way: "We can only be said to be alive in those moments when our hearts are conscious of our treasures; for our hearts are not strong enough to love every moment." Just to maintain consciousness of what could be—not necessarily to love it or live it, though this might happen occasionally, but just to be conscious.

Awareness, consciousness, sensing: these, I think, are the tools that will give us what we need—these coupled with desire and willingness. Scott Sanders, in *Staying Put,* explains: "All there is to see can be seen from anywhere in the universe, *if you know how to look;* and the influence of the entire universe converges on every spot." (Emphasis added)

What we need is to recognize that from where we are we can achieve satisfaction, the sense that comes from a beginning; from where we are we can feel the freshness of life continuing.

Beloved Community

The faith community called the church has always had a vision. The Unitarian Universalist vision is one of life in community as it could be, a community built on our seven principles. Preacher and prophet have spoken about the "Beloved Community," which is a phrase used in many congregations, including many Unitarian Universalist congregations. In Christian circles, people refer to the Kingdom of God or the Reign of God, which is that time, usually after life as we know it, when there will be equality, wholeness, and meaning for all people. In Unitarian Universalism, it's not that we don't believe in an afterlife, but our focus has always been on this life. The Beloved Community is what life could be like, right now, right here—not in some hereafter.

When we stand on the bridge of anti-oppression and intentionally name the demons of oppression and injustice, we are acknowledging that we will be committed to making the Beloved Community a reality and that it will only happen because we are committed and are willing to do the hard work that anti-oppression demands.

This was the vision that took me into the ministry, into the Unitarian Universalist Church. I have heard other Unitarian Universalist stories and visions too. I know it is something that is shared, it is a promise that inspires us. The Beloved Community—it is a journey toward wholeness.

Bible I

When I talk with people about whether or not they read the Bible and whether or not they have an appreciation for it, some of the answers I hear remind me of the young boy's response when his mother asked what he had learned in church school that day:

"The Israelites got out of Egypt, but Pharaoh and his army chased after them. They got to the Red Sea and they couldn't cross it. The Egyptian army was getting closer. So Moses got on his cell phone, the Israeli air force bombed the Egyptians, and the Israeli navy built a pontoon bridge so that people could cross." The mother was shocked. "Is that the way they taught you the story?" "Well, no," the boy admitted, "but if I told it to you the way they told it to us, you'd never believe it."

It's a common problem, an issue for many: how to understand, how to make sense of the Bible. Yet in spite of the difficulties that many may have with the Bible, it remains one of the most popular books—ever. I've read that every home in America has at least three Bibles! Granted, volume doesn't mean familiarity. Still, there's no denying that the book's popularity and durability are impressive.

But first things first—you need a Bible. If you are one of those with three or more, the problem could be choosing which one to read, since each could be a different English translation. You probably have at least one of two popular English translations. One is the King James Version (KJV), which was the first, making its appearance in 1611 and remaining for many the most authoritative source of God's word. For others, this authoritative-sounding language with all its thous and saiths is far from reality. Consequently, the chances are good that your other home Bible is the Revised Standard Version (RSV), first published in 1952. That means from 1611 to 1952, the KJV was *the* English translation, almost as sacred as the book itself! The RSV was an easier text to read and quickly became popular. During the 1950s and 1960s other translations surfaced, and maybe you have one of these, like the New English or the Jerusalem Bible. But beginning in the 1970s there was a proliferation of translations. *The Christian Century* reported: "We have the New American Bible, the Contemporary English Version, the New International, the New Revised, the Good News Bible as well as several hundred versions, catering to every niche of reader—from Bibles for runners and study books for teenagers to devotionals for mothers and couples, boys and girls."

Karl Barth once observed: "The Bible gives to every [person] and to every era such answers to their questions as they deserve. We shall always find in it as much as we seek and no more." The translation we choose to read can determine just how much we get from reading the Jewish and Christian Scriptures. What we get, what we are after when we absorb the word—what Barth says we deserve—can depend not only on what we're looking for, but on whether we let the Bible speak to us, whether we allow it to be a teacher.

We read the Bible to learn, to be inspired and moved. Like any of the world's sacred scriptures, the Bible has lessons to share with us if we are ready and willing to listen. The lessons come as poetry and prose, parable and fable, history and mythology, and speak to us on many levels. This certainly must be one of the most compelling reasons we want to read the biblical Scriptures: to hear the lessons, the perspective, and questions they offer.

What will it profit you if you gain the whole world and lose your soul? (Matthew 16:26)

What is truth? (John 18:38)
What do people gain from all the toil at which they toil
under the sun? (Ecclesiastes 1:3)
Where can I go from your spirit? Where can I flee from
your presence? (Psalms 139:7)
What shall I do to inherit eternal life? (Luke 10:25)
For everything there is a season and a time for every
purpose under heaven. (Ecclesiastes 3:1)
For where your treasure is, there your heart will be
also. (Matthew 6:21)
You are the light of the world. (Matthew 5:14)
(—New Revised Standard Version)

These are just a few of the affirmations, lessons, and
challenges that the Bible puts on our spiritual plate. For
personal instruction, for the questions asked of us and the
perspective we receive, for the deepening of our lives—
any one of these is a sufficient reason to read the Christian and Jewish Scriptures.

The Bible also speaks to us of social and ethical con-
cerns. The connection of Scripture lessons with belief
and behavior has always been strong. James told his congregation in Jerusalem:

What good is it, my brothers and sisters, if you say you
have faith but do not have works? Can faith save you? If a
brother or sister is naked and lacks daily food, and one of
you says to them: "Go in peace. Keep warm and eat your
fill," and yet you do not supply their bodily needs, what is
the good of that?
So faith by itself, if it has no works, is dead. Show me
your faith apart from your works, and I by my works will
show you my faith. (James 2:14–17, 18b)

James, like Jesus, was a Jew. The Jewish imperative
of living your faith was as strong then as it is today. Rabbi
Harold Kushner tells us:

I believe there is a straight line from the biblical story
of the Exodus to contemporary Jewish involvement in is-

sues of social justice. Remembering, and annually repeating, the story of slavery and liberation, we have developed a sense of empathy for the oppressed. In a museum exhibit between Jews and blacks, I found the following quotation from a woman named Sabrina Virgo:

"When I was young, I was taught that Jewish meant: you don't cross picket lines, you work for peace, you fight for social justice, you never forget the suffering of your people as a line to the suffering of others." (*To Life!*)

In our Unitarian Universalist Principles and Purposes, it reads: "The living tradition we share draws from many sources," among them "Jewish and Christian teachings which call us to respond to God's love by loving our neighbors as ourselves." The ethical imperative, as Kushner suggests, is clear and strong in our heritage:

Am I my brother's keeper? (Genesis 4:9)

Let anyone among you who is without sin be the first to throw a stone. (John 8:7)

They shall beat their swords into plowshares and their spears into pruning hooks; nation shall not lift up sword against nation, neither shall they learn war any more. (Isaiah 2:4)

Blessed are the peace-makers for they shall be called children of God. (Matthew 5:9)

The beginning of wisdom is this: Get wisdom, get insight . . . Keep hold of instruction; do not let go; guard her, for she is your life. (Proverbs 4:7, 13)

Faith, hope and love—these three abide, but the greatest of these is love. (I Corinthians 13:13)

[What is required of you is] to do justice, love kindness and to walk humbly with your God. (Micah 6:8)

You shall love your neighbor as yourself. (Mark 12:31)

The personal and social teachings in both the Hebrew and Christian Scriptures are too important to ignore. The questions they ask us to examine, the discussions they urge us to begin, the challenge and support they give are simply too good to pass up.

Ours is a biblically interested nation, a Bible-rooted culture—there's no getting away from this fact. Unfamiliarity with the Scriptures puts any person at a loss. Biblical illustrations, quotes, references, and sources are in the fabric of our culture, whether in jokes, stories, literature, the theater, political speeches, movies—you name it, everywhere there are Bible references. To understand our culture, you have to have some familiarity with these Scriptures.

Finally, we should read the Bible because there are some who are fond of quoting the Scriptures to justify their social and political pronouncements: it's important to know whether or not what they've said is correct. For example, when the Gospels (or sayings of Jesus) are used to condemn abortion or homosexuality, you need to know that nowhere in the Gospels does Jesus or anyone else ever say anything about either subject: Jesus is mute on the topics. You need to now that if anyone ever refers to the Hebrew Scriptures prohibiting homosexuality or abortion, or claims that they speak to other current issues, it's likely that they are citing the book of Leviticus or Deuteronomy, where you can also find prohibitions on virtually anything—like clothing composed of blends—or how about advice on getting the perfect wife: find an attractive prisoner of war, bring her home, shave her head, trim her nails, and give her some new clothes. Then she's yours (Deut. 21: 11–13). Of course when it comes to theology, every Unitarian Universalist must know that nowhere in the Gospels does it ever say anything about a trinity; after all, these people were Jews! And for all those who advocate public prayer as biblically based, remember what Jesus told his followers: "When you pray, you must not be like the hypocrites, for they love to stand and pray . . . they like to be seen by others. . . . But when you go into your room and shut the door, pray to your Father who is in secret." (Matthew 6: 5–6)

There's a lot that's done and supported in politics, in the name of family values, in the name of all people of the scriptural heritage. Read the Bible so you know what's accurate.

Mark Twain had this advice: "Most people are bothered by those passages in Scripture which they cannot understand; but as for me, I always notice that the passages in Scripture which trouble me most are those which I do understand." Why read the Bible? We too can be moved, and challenged to seek clarity, a deeper understanding of ourselves and others; we read the Bible because it is poetry and prose, story and fable, history and mythology. It is our story in all its glory and corruption, beauty and confusion, serenity and violence. This is the story of humankind. Read the Bible to understand and know who we are, where we have been, and where we might be going.

Bible II

Sixty-six books: thirty-nine in the Hebrew Scriptures, twenty-seven in the Christian. Hundreds of English translations, but in the King James Version it comes out to 773,746 words. It's not surprising that many have chosen to be selective about what they read in the Bible: there's a lot to cover and not all of it is relevant, clear, or appropriate. It was Ralph Waldo Emerson who suggested: "Make your own Bible. Select and collect all the words and sentences that in your reading have been like the blast of triumph out of Shakespeare, Seneca, Moses, John and Paul."

This is what Thomas Jefferson did years earlier. Jefferson "cut and pasted" his own bible, so it included only the teaching and sayings of Jesus; he eliminated all the miracles and stories. Years after Emerson offered up his advice, Unitarian feminist Elizabeth Cady Stanton published her version of the Christian Scriptures as she believed they embraced all people—not just white men.

Jefferson, Emerson, and Stanton were thinking and acting in good Unitarian Universalist fashion, relying on that authority they new best—their own experience. Ultimately, individual or collective experience is the determining factor. Each of us is our own authority when reading the Bible; we read the Scriptures from our own experience or context. When an African-American, a Latino, or an Asian, a man or a woman, a gay, lesbian, bisexual, or straight reads the scriptural texts, their experience and context shape their understanding. To have a well-rounded appreciation of the Scriptures, you'll need a sense of what they look like through these different lenses of understanding. Sometimes, when you read through another's lens, not only will your appreciation be fuller, but you can be moved beyond appreciation to fundamental change.

How should we read the Bible? One way is with a contextual understanding, recognizing that your reading of the Scriptures will be influenced by who and where you are and what it is that you bring to the text, which in all likelihood will not be what every person will bring to their reading.

I find it hard to read the Bible alone—maybe a first reading of course, but after that I find it much richer when I'm with others. So a second way to read the Bible is with a group. A few years ago I was taking a class on the book of Job. There was quite a bit of reading from the text and commentaries that had to be done before class. But my reading wasn't nearly as meaningful as the class discussion, which was filled with insights, meaning, and lessons I could never have developed on my own. The class was composed of laity and clergy, men and women, African-America, Asian, European and North Atlantic, Christian, Jew, and three Unitarian Universalists. I could never get alone what I received in that group of twenty. The contexts and interpretations were abundant and often powerful.

So I recommend that another way to read the Bible is with a group: first alone, but then with others who wish to explore the text with you—its lessons and insights—for personal, spiritual meanings and ethical value.

And finally, a dilemma: whether to read the Bible as it is written or with what we know today. There are three ways to approach this choice. First, virtually everything we read has been written in a particular style and it's all different: fiction or nonfiction, poetry or prose, story or tale, borrowed or original, firsthand or second- (third- or fourth-), history or mythology. When we read a book or a magazine, we know what we're reading, we know either from the author, from the style in which it's written, or even from its classification at the library. The biblical texts also are composed of all these different kinds of literary styles, and to think that it's all literal, firsthand history is as wrong as it would be to think of it all as borrowed mythology. Therefore it can be clarifying to know what is what, and to do that you're going to have to read more than what's presented in the chapter and verse.

Second, the Jewish and Christian Middle Eastern cultures that produced the Scriptures had an attitude toward history and the recording of history that is far different from what we expect from our historians. It wasn't uncommon for writers of that time to attribute direct quotes to a person based on what they likely had said. It was just assumed that, for example, since a person was a middle-aged, Jewish male from central Israel living under Roman rule, such a person might say this or that. Such sloppy historical recording and speculation wouldn't be tolerated today, but then it was okay. So, we have to keep in mind that what we read in the Scriptures is far from an accurate recording of what people said.

Third, the social conditions that produced the Scriptures—their lessons and value—are not identical to our experiences. For example, one person talks about the way that American slave-owners often cited biblical Scripture as justification for holding slaves. As reported in *The Christian Century:*

> But slavery in ancient Israel was a very different sort of institution. It was not based on race. Many slaves were supposed to be freed at the end of seven years, and there was a good bit of movement back and forth between slavery and freedom. Israelite slavery may have been a bad institution, but it was a very different institution from that of American slavery. It was more like the hiring of indentured servants, if one wants an American analogy. So one can't simply transfer what the bible says about 'slavery' to an American context where the institution and the circumstances are very different and the word therefore has a different meaning.

So, before you draw contemporary parallels from the Bible, as you listen to others do the same, remember that it often doesn't work, it's not that easy. All of this understanding about the social, historical, cultural, and literary backgrounds becomes very important when learning how to read the Bible. Without an awareness of these possibilities, it's easy to get distracted and stray away from what the writers had hoped to share.

If you read the Scriptures with a closed mind, if you read the Bible wondering if everything really happened like it says or if you read it wondering "Is it true?" then your search and your learning will be frustrating, maybe fruitless. You see, there comes a time in reading Scripture—any religious scripture, not only the Bible— when the questions that come so easily have to be shelved, set aside, so that insights can occur, so your prejudices won't block the lessons and insights that are larger than the words. The questions come so effortlessly to our educated minds.

You can read the Bible with a critical, enlightened mind, but you have to remember at least two things: First, trying to read the Scriptures as though they were a moral, philosophical, or historical textbook for the twenty-first century is a burden we have chosen to place on it. It's hard to believe that its authors had this kind of longevity in mind when they wrote what they did or when the Bible was assembled and ordered.

Second, I encourage you to read the Scriptures, ponder its lessons and stories and history, argue with it, challenge it, learn from it, but it should never become any person's single source of inspiration or education. There's a bigger picture to keep in mind, and perhaps it's in the tension between religious Scripture (or religious discipline) and this wider view—it's here where the deepening and completing of life is begun, challenged, and lived.

At the conclusion of *Resurrection: Myth or Reality?* his fourteenth book on scriptural issues and themes, this is the way Bishop John Spong says it:

I will never again seek to speculate on the nature of life
after death, the definition of heaven, or the arguments for
or against its reality. Those books I read in my earlier life
will remain in a row on a shelf in my library. I will not open
them again. . . . This is not my business. My business is to
live now, to love now, and to be now.

So let us live, my brothers and sisters. Let us even eat,
drink and be merry, not because tomorrow we shall die but
because today we are alive and it is our vocation to be
alive—to be alive to [our] God, alive to ourselves.

"To be alive to [our] God, and to ourselves." It's for this
that the whys and the hows of reading religious Scripture
serve us. If this is not its value, if this is not its challenge,
then go elsewhere until you find it. "To be alive to [our]
God, alive to ourselves." This is the meaning of Scripture
and religion, of living. This is why and how to read the
Bible.

Born Again

As Christians tell it and as I understand it, being born again means that you've had a life-altering, transforming, Holy Spirit-induced experience which has either brought you to claiming Jesus as your Lord or powerfully reaffirmed and reconfirmed your being a Christian. Being born a second time is like seeing life through new eyes, eyes washed by the Holy Spirit, with the blood of Christ. Now you know your sins have been forgiven, now you can feel the difference—you have been saved!

For at least 80 percent of us, given our non-Unitarian Universalist background, and sometimes with a potpourri of tumultuous feelings for and suspicions about organized religion, we can assert that a common characteristic among us is that we are at least twice-born. Like the fundamentalist, we too have been born again! Fundamentalist Christians don't have a monopoly on religious rebirth. In fact, I think that being twice-born is a fairly common experience among Unitarian Universalists—it's just that we've never had the language to describe the experience.

This is what I mean: It's not rebirth as in the popular notion of conversion. Conversion in both Greek and Hebrew does not mean *rebirth* but *turning*. I like to think of it as Carol Christ does: "awakening." She writes: "To one [awakened], it is as if she had been trying to make out clear shapes in a dark room and suddenly the lights were turned on." (*Diving Deep and Surfacing*)

So, how are we religious liberals awakened, twice-born, or, if you prefer the more familiar language, how is it that we come to be born again? There are at least three ways. Let me start with a story:

A carpenter and his apprentice were walking together through a large forest. When they came across a tall, huge, gnarled, old, beautiful oak tree, the carpenter asked his apprentice: "Do you know why this tree is so tall, so huge, so gnarled, so old and beautiful?" The apprentice looked at his master and said: "No, why?" "Well," the carpenter said, "because it is useless. If it had been useful it would have been cut long ago and made into tables and chairs, but because it is useless it could grow so tall and so beautiful that you can sit in its shade and relax."

The trick to being twice-born is not in being chosen, elected, blessed, or saying-all-the-right-words-at-all-the-right-times-because-you're-in-all-the-right-places. Being awaked, born again, for even the third or fourth time, comes from seeing the old, gnarled, beautiful tree for what it is; it comes in taking the time to step back and seeing things as if new; it comes from open eyes and liberal feelings; it comes from seeing the extraordinary in the very ordinary.

Another way I see Unitarian Universalists being twice born is acknowledging that too often in religion we take as the literal truth what needs to be understood metaphorically or symbolically. This does not imply a loss of meaning or power. There merely needs to be a suspension of belief which then creates an opportunity for us to see what is truly there—to see with the lights turned out.

Unfortunately, both liberals and conservatives can become narrow and unbending in their belief systems. I'm reminded of the story that Peter Fleck tells about Benjamin:

> Benjamin, when he was 4 years old, lived in Iowa, and though he didn't live on a farm, he had an imaginary farm. From time to time he told his parents what was going on there. One day he said to his mother: "Mom, you know what

happened last night? Last night the vet came and you know what he did? He cut a little piece off the hoof of the cow and now she has a calf." His mother, who had a talent for seizing opportunities when they present themselves, felt that this was the moment to introduce her son to the facts of life. And then she embarked on a long story about how a little calf is really made. "You see Benjamin," she said in the end, "that is how it really happens." Whereupon Benjamin looked her straight in the eye and said: "Not on *my* farm!"
(*The Blessings of Imperfection*)

Like Benjamin, we can fall into the trap of parochialism. In its clutches so much is closed out, so much is never given the opportunity for exploration, for touching us. There's an uncompromising rigidity of belief in saying, "Not on *my* farm!" or in turning the metaphoric and mythological into the truth. It's a rigidity that guarantees that no new experiences can possibly happen.

The Unitarian Universalists who have shared their awakening with me, of how they are twice-born, all seem to nurture and in this sense welcome the unexpected, the symbolic, the opportunity to see with a new set of glasses. There's sound advice in the "Peanuts" cartoon that shows Snoopy atop his doghouse at the typewriter. Charlie Brown says to him: "I hear you're writing a book on theology . . . I hope you have a good title." Snoopy confidently thinks: "I have the perfect title . . . 'Has It Ever Occurred to You That You Might Be Wrong?'"

I've been wrong so many times that I don't have enough fingers to count it out. Each time I've been wrong has been a chance to be born again. Unitarian Universalists seem to thrive on getting up close and personal with the loss of faith and doubt. And it's in this where I see another opportunity for awakening at its deepest level, an experiential one.

I like the sentiment in this statement: "Tell me and I'll forget. Show me and I may not remember. Involve me and I'll understand." Bill Schulz once said that we have a "Theology of Dirty Hands" (UUA pamphlet on social justice). So what if we tend to be kind of messy—great!

Wonderful! It's when we're dirty, doubting, and downcast that we create chance of being twice-born, for seeing, feeling, and believing in new ways.

Now, if you have a hard time believing that religious liberals can be born again, listen to the way that Harold Kushner writes about it:

> William James's twice-born souls are people who lose their faith and then regain it, but their new faith is very different from the one they lost. Instead of seeing a world flooded with sunshine, as the once-born always do, they see a world where the sun struggles to come out after the storm but always manages to reappear. . . . And like the bone that breaks and heals stronger at the broken place, like the string that is stronger where it broke and was knotted, it is a stronger faith than it was before, because it has learned it can survive the loss of faith. (*Who Needs God*)

Call it born again, twice born, a turning, or an awakening, they all name the same experience—a temporary malaise or loss of faith, a period of doubt, a time of profound questioning. And in this window of confusion, even meaninglessness, is an opportunity that might be neglected at first, but then is seized, kindled, embraced—and then finally you are born again!

Christmas

Would Jesus celebrate Christmas, his birthday? I propose three ways to go about answering this question.

First, look at what Jesus and his contemporaries, his family, might have been doing on December 25. This, in fact, might be the most honest answer to this question. Another way to look at it might be to wonder: Before there was a Christmas, before there was a Jesus Christ, what was happening? What was the world like, the world into which Jesus was born?

Another possible way to look at the question: What did the early church do for "His Birthday"? These were Jesus' family, friends, and followers and I suppose you could argue that since they were the closest to him they might have some insight and understanding that have escaped us. So there is something to learn from them, or even the institutional church that followed. As we go back, closer to the actual event, peeling away layers and layers of history, you'd think we might get closer to the truth.

Third, I wonder what Jesus might say about the church's observance and celebration of his birthday as we have come to know it. We can only guess, and often do, how he might respond to the cultural Christmas that has grown up around the twenty-fifth—every year there are op-ed diatribes, magazine articles, and sermons from every Christian faith community seeking a more simple, more meaningful, more Christlike holiday.

And that's just the point of this historical and faith exercise. What does it mean to have a more Christlike holiday? From my earliest recollections I remember people talking about the corruption of Christmas, of putting Christ back into Christmas, of how commercialism had ruined what I always thought, as a child, was a wonderful event. "Oh, to return to a simpler day when Christmas was meaningful," I would hear grownups groan (and evidently, according to Stephen Nissenbaum in *The Battle for Christmas,* it's been a mantra among adults since at least the 1840s).

Would Jesus celebrate Christmas? Would he observe his birthday? Let's see.

There are at least two things that we do know for sure. First, Jesus was Jewish, and second, his homeland was occupied territory. As a Jew, would Jesus and his family observe Hanukkah during December? Remember that unlike the Christmas, Hanukkah moves anywhere from late November to late December, and it lasts for eight days. But Hanukkah is not only considered a minor religious observance but it was not always observed because of embarrassment: after the Maccabees defeated their oppressors, they eventually became as corrupt and oppressive. Those who had supported and believed in them, especially the rabbis, were distraught and embarrassed as their nation fell apart, and finally, once again, fell under foreign domination. Jesus might have observed a version of what we now recognize as Hanukkah, but I doubt it.

It's far more likely that Jesus, his family, and their faith community were, like everyone else, caught in the tug and pull of competing political, cultural, and religious ideologies that might make even our diversity-conscious heads spin. Remember that stories similar to what we would eventually recognize as the Christ story were abundant in his days. Quoting Peter Samson, Jean Schramm's description (*Church of the Larger Fellowship Newsletter*) of the birth, life, and worship of Zoroaster who lived six centuries before Jesus is a perfect example of what I

mean. Zoroastrian followers were still active in his day.
And this is just the beginning of the religious potpourri:

> It is fascinating to reflect that the time which finally be-
> came the birthday of Jesus also happened to be the birth
> time of Hercules, who was born of a virgin; of Krishna, the
> incarnate Hindu god who was born of a virgin mother in a
> cave while shepherds watched their flocks and his parents
> fled a wicked king; of Bacchus, or Dionysos, who was born
> of a virgin and Zeus; of Tammuz, the god of the Assyrians
> and the Babylonians, who was born of a virgin and Attis, the
> Phrygian sun god.

And let's not forget that this was Roman territory and
an agrarian society, and versions of Roman pagan-nature
observances and beliefs permeated almost everything.
Topping the list was Saturnalia, which many say is the
historical Christmas. Saturnalia was a week-long bash of
merry-making, sex, and drunkenness to celebrate the
birthday of the Sun, actually the so-called return of the
sun. The seven days of Saturnalia saw gift-giving and
equality among all people, and finally culminated on the
twenty-fifth, the day Romans believed was the shortest
of the year.

All of this, then, is what filled the lives of Jews around
the time of Jesus' birth. Jesus would have been born into
it. To what extent people had to participate in one observance or another I don't know; to what extent Jews were
left alone to practice their faith, I don't know. What we do
know is how easily a small faith community, as Jews were
on his birthday, can be pushed, shoved, manipulated, and
transformed by a dominant culture. I mean, just based on
our own experience as Unitarian Universalists and from
watching or participating in Judaism, we can feel or know
how orthodox Christian dogma can take over and nearly
drown out all of the other voices. It must have been similar for Jesus' tiny Jewish community, who had to live
among the tug-of-war of all the different ideologies and
theologies under Roman occupation.

Would Jesus celebrate Christmas, his birthday? Historically, the simple answer is no, because Jews considered birthdays heathen recognitions and not part of Jewish practice. But living in such a multicultural, diverse, religiously and politically explosive setting, Jesus must have been aware of his birthday, and if only in his mind, have paused to note it.

And still, we have no idea when Jesus was born. With no clues to be found in the Gospel narratives, early church fathers of the third century placed his birth on May 20 and others on April 19 or 20. Clement, Bishop of Alexandria (died c. 215), nominated November 18. Hippolytus (died c. 236) calculated that Christ must have been born on Wednesday, the same day God created the sun. Another church leader posited that the first day of creation coincided with the first day of spring, on March 25, and contended that Jesus's birthday fell three days later, on March 28. All of these dates and any other ones are merely speculative best guesses.

What we do know, and what is quite clear, is that in the years after Jesus' death his followers had absolutely no interest in knowing his birthdate because they anticipated the end of the world and his return; why should they bother with a birthdate when they believed he'd never died? But we also know that as the years peeled away, Jesus didn't return and the end of the world didn't come, and early theologians like Paul had to create new reasons for staying loyal to the faith. It was then that learning more about the nativity grew important. But it was too late—no one remembered the month or day.

Sometime in the early years of the fourth century, Christianity had grown enough and felt secure enough to challenge all the other cultural and religious traditions that filled the times, many of them the same observances that had filled the life and mind of Jesus. In one of the most astute moves ever, one that would characterize Christianity's growth until today, their leaders chose to appropriate popular, ongoing holidays and piggyback on them. And that's the way December 25 was chosen. Hav-

ing no idea when Jesus was born, the early chur
lected the last day of Saturnalia as fitting for their observance. In this way, they could indirectly challenge Roman
authority and paganism, and also make less clear who
was celebrating what event, thus creating the illusion
that there might be far more Christians than anyone realized. The scales were finally tipped in the middle of the
fourth century when Roman Emperor Constantine con-
verted to Christianity, and in a symbolic act of conversion
and loyalty he built the Vatican atop the hill where sun
worshippers may have gathered.

On the surface, Christmas is to Christianity as
Hanukkah is to Judaism—an important but peripheral
recognition. On the other hand, Christianity's Easter and
the High Holy Days of Judaism are quintessential events
in the life of these faith communities. You see, the Christian message is meaningless without death and resurrection. Or as I heard one person put it, no one ever waits
outside a delivery room expecting the birth of a great person, meaning that Jesus did not become an important figure at birth, but only at death. Christmas has become a
significant date because of who Jesus became and how he
died, which is what Easter is all about. It's in this sense
that the Puritans were theologically right when they
chose to ignore Christmas—in fact, as long as they were
in power Christmas was outlawed! It was sacrilegious to
observe Christmas.

All of this is simply to say that if we look at the meaning and message of the early Christian church, there is
no lessening of the Christmas confusion. With each
decade and then century after Jesus' crucifixion, the
confusion deepened and the story grew to a point that
had Jesus returned, he would never have recognized his
own birth narrative.

Imagine someone telling you the story of your birth
and having very little of it—maybe even none of it—sound
remotely plausible or familiar. This is what Jesus would
have found within a couple of centuries of his death and
certainly today. To put it bluntly, the Gospel biographies—

all of them—are wrong: they are make-believe stories, stories created and told for particular audiences. This is why no two of the stories are the same and why it's impossible that they are parts of the same story. And what's amazing is that, while few us could recognize this without help from outside sources, Jesus, because he was Jewish, would recognize it immediately. For example, both the Matthew and Luke narratives, the ones always used, are full of references to Hebrew scripture that all Jews would have recognized and valued. And why did they include these? Because they were trying to persuade Jewish audiences that Jesus was the Messiah, the new David, the King of Kings. And so they pulled out sacred scriptural stories and references that they knew their audience would be familiar with, stories and references that would "prove" Jesus was the Son of God. Those birth narratives were not written for us, they are not descriptive of his birthday, they are as fictional as any of the other ancient myths we've read. I imagine Jesus laughing and laughing if he heard these stories—they are so far from historical reality, a reality that we can only speculate about.

But they are great stories, historically flawed though they might be. And when coupled with the yuletide mythology that is part of the secular world, the result is a December 25 that would be unrecognizable to Jesus, his followers, or any of the early Christians of the first century.

While the biblical narratives are story and the very finest of fiction, the hopes, disappointments, dreams, and disillusionment that they speak about are very real. While written for Jewish ears and eyes, they also speak to the hearts and spirit of all people. This is why they are so appealing: they strike chords that resonate throughout the ages, beyond time, ethnicity, gender, and culture.

In the quiet of reflection about the Christmas season, if you have the ear to hear and heart to feel, you will be able to know Emmanuel—God within. If this is what the Christmas season is about, if finding Emmanuel within yourself and each other is what his birthday means, then yes, Jesus probably would celebrate Christmas.

Covenant

The last paragraph of our Unitarian Universalist Principles and Purposes is the mission statement of the UUA. *Mission* names our purpose; mission tells what we do and why:

> The Unitarian Universalist Association shall devote its resources to and exercise its corporate powers for religious, educational, and humanitarian purposes. The primary purpose of the Association is to serve the needs of its member congregations, organize new congregations, extend and strengthen Unitarian Universalist institutions, and implement its principles.

Next, we see that as a "member congregation of the UUA, we covenant to affirm and promote . . ." and then the seven principles are named. Often people mistake these Principles as our covenant, but they are not. The Principles state our ideal, the Principles are a picture of what we want. It is our Association's vision—a vision of the Beloved Community.

So what is our covenant? We are a covenantal faith, not a creedal one. Most of us who come to Unitarian Universalism from other faith communities probably come from creedal faiths: faiths that are centered around a creed, a statement of beliefs that everyone acknowledges and accepts. The creed is recited by the congregation during their worship; it's the creed that binds the congregation together. We are a creedless faith; we are bound not by creed, but by covenant. A covenant is the commitments and promises that we voluntarily make to each other. At the end of the Principles and Purposes is our Association's covenant: "As free congregations we enter into this covenant, *promising to one another our mutual trust and support.*"

Mission and vision can be found in virtually every congregation of any faith. While the words and specifics of our mission and vision could be unique to us, there is nothing on the surface that makes them Unitarian Universalist; I know of many congregations that have similar goals and ideals.

No, not mission and vision, but covenant is what makes us unique. Covenant is the how and the why that gives power to our mission and vision. And it's covenant that makes everything else uniquely Unitarian Universalist. Whether it's an annual canvass or a capital fund drive, teaching religious education or creating adult enrichment, attending morning worship, mindfulness meditation, or an earth-centered ritual, landscaping the grounds, singing in the choir or volunteering in the office—these, and everything else we do, are grounded in covenant, in the voluntary promises and commitments we make to each other. It's covenant that makes us Unitarian Universalists: we are a covenantal faith.

As glorious and appealing as the mission and vision are, these are not what we promise and commit to. What we promise and commit to is "mutual trust and support." Our covenant is grounded in community, in being together. One radical implication of this is that it's impossible to be a Unitarian Universalist alone. I have a friend whose parents left their Unitarian Universalist church after the congregation undertook a building program they didn't agree with; they were dissatisfied with the direction the church was going. (I'm always suspicious of people who resign their membership over polity issues—it seems to become a convenient place to hang their hat of dissatisfaction.) This husband and wife never joined any other Unitarian Universalist congregation. Yet they still identify themselves as Unitarian Universalist. I submit that that's not possible because the nature of our faith is not creedal—just because you agree with mission and vision doesn't mean you're a Unitarian Universalist. The essence of our faith is covenantal: you must be in relationship with other Unitarian Universalists—you can't do it alone. The only way to be a Unitarian Universalist is to be part of a Unitarian Universalist congregation, to make promises and commitments around vision and mission.

The current cultural trends seem to indicate that religious community is not popular. There's a suspicion of institutions and I can understand that. Often we get invested in institutions and then feel betrayed when something doesn't go the way we feel it should. Instead of faith communities, people are into spirituality, following their unique individual spiritual path—it's an individualistic course of action instead of a community one.

I know that many Unitarian Universalists feel the tension created by the paths of community and individualism. This tension has been part of our historical faith tradition for centuries. In fact, the early Christian church was divided over the same kinds of issues and probably every faith tradition has been challenged by this apparent chasm. Life itself presents us with two options: one of enjoying the world, which is often done personally and individually, and one of improving the world, which is often done with others, in community, by commitment and promise. And, as E.B. White suggests, we arise many mornings torn over how to plan our day—whether to enjoy it or improve it.

At its best, this balancing can be done in covenant—I think that our vision and mission speak about both individual and community needs, they speak of enjoying and improving. These are not mutually exclusive categories, but rather need to be balanced. In our communites, we covenant to do both.

Death

As a faith without a dogma, there is no official Unitarian Universalist belief about death, life after death, or anything of this sort. At the same time, having hung around with Unitarian Universalists for more than twenty-five years, I have a vague idea of what the majority might believe. So while it's accurate to say that we don't have an authoritative dogma-like belief about death, it's not fair to say that we don't have a theology of death. It actually might be more accurate to say that we have theolog*ies* of death.

There's a Hasidic story that puts this in perspective. It's told that as a rabbi lay dying, his wife at his bedside broke into tears. "But why are you crying?" he asked. "My whole life was only that I might learn how to die." Is it too much to ask that in a lifetime we might develop a philosophy of death? Certainly it isn't too much to ask that our religious faith be an important contributor, shaper, provider in our learning how to die.

Our philosophy of death can't be viewed in isolation, but only in the context of religious, family, and school teaching and discussion as well as from the experiences we've had in our lifetime, experiences of every sort. Who knows what finally emerges as significant—the stillborn birth of a kitten at four and your mother's explanation; a mouse crushed in a trap and your father's reasoning; the sickness and death of a classmate in junior high and your best friend's spin on it all. To this day I remember the sights, sounds, and smells when at fifteen I attended, by

myself, the wake for a high school friend killed in
cident. At twenty-five, forty-five, or eighty-five, al~ ~~ ~~~
could still have a profound and lasting impact on even the
most rational and logical of adult philosophies.

As children, as young adults, I'm sure you were a lot
like me: virtually nothing was impossible, the sky was
the limit, and while I may not have thought I would live
forever, I sure didn't give much thought to death. The
things I did, the places I put my energy, my lifestyle,
which is all to say my priorities, showed little, if any,
recognition that life and time were limited. I was taking
some pretty big scoops from the cookie jar, a jar that appeared virtually endless with pleasure and gratification.
I'm reminded of a "Peanuts" cartoon that shows Charlie
and Linus standing in front of an inches-high sapling.
Charlie says: "It's a beautiful little tree. Isn't it?" "Yes, it
is," responds Linus. Charlie says: "It's a shame that we
won't be around to see it when it's fully grown." To which
Linus asks: "Why? Where are we going?" Such is the perspective of youth.

Getting older, I understand what Charlie is talking
about—I know I am going somewhere and won't be
around to watch the sapling reach maturity. While I still
can't see the bottom of the jar, I know it's there, and that
the contents won't last forever. This doesn't mean that I
quit taking risks, that I stop taking pleasure in life, it
doesn't mean to stop and take it easy; but it does push me
to ask a new question. Instead of wondering what else in
life there is for me to take on, I now wonder: "What am I
doing with my life?" It's the recognition that in living well,
we are preparing to die well. It's the recognition that
there is continuity between living and dying, and the way
to prepare for a good death is with a good life.

I have read that we each have three wishes at our
death. While we may have quite a few more, I think that
these three are good ones, if for no other reason (and there
are many other reasons) than they give direction for living well. That is to say, they are death wishes that must
be acted out in life.

First, at your death you would hope that your friends and family, those here and those you've had contact with over your life, would know what you meant by your life. In other words, you hope they know how you would want to be remembered. Of course, the beauty of this wish, as well as the others to follow, is that it's quite simple to act upon. You just have to live what you mean, you simply have to "walk your talk," or, as Albert Schweitzer boldly put it, you must "make your life your argument."

A second wish: that when you die, you would hope that you'd made a difference, that you had left behind something of yourself that had made a difference. In order to make the kind of difference that we wish for, we must learn the lesson taught by Harold Kushner, who tells of this experience:

> I was sitting on a beach one summer day, watching two children, a boy and a girl, playing in the sand. They were hard at work building an elaborate sand castle by the water's edge, with gates and towers and moats and internal passages. Just when they had nearly finished their project, a big wave came along and knocked it down, reducing it to a heap of wet sand. I expected the children to burst into tears, devastated by what had happened to all their hard work. But they surprised me. Instead, they ran up the shore away from the water, laughing and holding hands, and sat down to build another castle. I realized that they had taught me an important lesson. All the things in our lives, all the complicated structures we spend so much time and energy creating, are built on sand. Only our relationships to other people endure. Sooner or later, the wave will come along and knock down what we have worked so hard to build up. When that happens, only the person who has somebody's hand to hold will be able to laugh. (*When All You've Ever Wanted Isn't Enough*)

If when you die you wish to be remembered for having made a difference, it must be done through and with people—holding hands, walking shoulder to shoulder, laughing and crying, shouting and dancing together. The more there are, the richer will be your experience. Anything other than this will risk the wave of time destroying the castles that crumble like sand.

Finally, a third wish: that those you love not be confused or hurt, but ready to carry on in your absence with courage and fortitude. I have seen countless times when a person who has died has left those behind in crisis because they have no idea what is to be done, where important papers might be, the estate is a mess and/or a secret. All focus is thus taken away from bereavement, healing, and reflection and placed on making order out of chaos. This is largely avoidable; it does not have to happen. I wonder how many have talked with their partner, their family, or their friends about what they expect to happen at their death—what they expect to happen to their body, with their property; I wonder how many have taken the time to smooth out—as much as possible—any difficulties there might be among family members and friends, so that when they die additional strains aren't placed on those they love. I wonder how many have a will, have contacted a funeral home or memorial society, have made sure their partner, family, and close friends understand what they mean by their desires. I wonder how many have thought through the constellation of issues which at their death someone else will be asked to resolve. If at your death it is your wish that those you love and care about not be confused or lost but have the courage to carry on in your absence, then you had better make sure that they will have the opportunity to fulfill that wish.

These aren't the kinds of things we learn from family or school, nor unfortunately from church. Actually, they never taught us anything of this sort in seminary—we never even discussed learning to die by learning to live. Everything I've learned has been through "on the job training," and often in the most unique of settings. For example, it was in my second year of seminary that I performed my first graveside burial—and like many deaths and funerals, it was unexpected but reflected all the issues that I now, decades later, have experienced as commonplace. I was working at a very small German Lutheran church in the Bronx, running an after-school center for neighborhood kids—the congregation's attempt to reach out into the community. It was fall and the weather still permitted us to use the property behind the church building.

One afternoon I heard shouts of shock, alarm, and excitement: "Mr. Muir, Mr. Muir. Come here. Come right now!" I went running to where I heard the voices, not knowing what I'd find. A group of kids were standing next to the building in a semicircle staring at the ground. "What's up guys?" I said as I approached. There, next to the building, at their feet, was one very dead rat. Not really sure what to do myself, I nudged the body with my foot and sure enough, it was dead and very stiff.

"Somebody run inside and get me a trash bag," I said. "A trash bag?" somebody asked. "We can't bury it in a trash bag." "Bury it?!" I said. "Bury it!? We aren't. . . ." But no sooner had I begun to try to explain how we would simply throw it in the city trash collection than one of the kids said they knew where a shoe box was, and someone else knew where there was some soft stuffing for inside the box, and another kid said she was pretty sure she knew where the rat had been living. And of course, said one more: "Mr. Muir will do whatever needs to be done. Won't you Mr. Muir?"

By then, some of the kids had gone back to the yard searching for a fitting burial site, others were rummaging through the church offices looking for anything and everything that would create the proper ambiance for the occasion, and a few had left the property to spread the news among the other neighborhood children to assemble at the church, all of which left me standing alone with the deceased rodent wondering what to say and what to do if the church's pastor got wind of the afternoon's events (which was a literal possibility to be determined by the digging ability of the self-appointed burial team).

Eventually, we managed to get the rat into the box, though on the way to the gravesite it was nearly dropped several times since there were always four pallbearers

with as many waiting their turn. About twenty-f
showed up for the ceremony and I—well, I wasn
sure what to say, and actually, I don't remember what I
did say. But I do know that it all came off without a hitch.
Apparently, everyone had their needs met.

The really amazing thing about this story, and perhaps the great lesson for me as a second-year seminarian
along with its value for the children involved, was that it
held within it many—maybe all—of the pieces that you'd
find and experience with the death of any person: shock
and alarm, denial and celebration, notification of friends
and family, planning and preparation, people who want to
do nothing and people who want to do everything, the disruption of everyday routines, indecision and spontaneity,
and more—I mean, it was all there!

We are going to die. But will we die focused on dying
or will we die living, so when our time comes—and come
it will—our friends and family will know what we meant
with our lives; we'll die knowing we made a difference;
and we'll die knowing that we prepared our families and
friends as best we could. For in doing these things, we will
die living, which is what the writer in Deuteronomy recalls God promising: "I have set before you life and death,
blessings and curses. Choose life so that you and your de-
scendants may live." (30:19)

Demons

In Paul's letter to the Christians of Corinth, who were having some tough times and needed his support, he counsels: "But God chose the foolish things of the world to confound the wise; and God chose the weak things of the world to confound the mighty." (1 Corinthians 1:27) This is the biblical version of a radio and TV announcement that I'm sure you're familiar with: "This is a test. Please do not adjust your dial. This is only a test." Don't fuss with the reception. What you're receiving is accurate, as far as it goes. Don't be fooled by appearances because there is more, clarity will emerge; completeness will follow, if you are willing to wait and discover it.

A therapist once told me almost the same thing. I was curious about some of the characters in my dreams. For instance, I had a dream set in the church I served in Maine. The congregation was there, it must have been a Sunday, and I was in the front row, watching the minister, not me, perform a whole series of pastoral acts—a child dedication, a wedding, welcoming newcomers. But the minister was dressed as a clown and there was a carnival-circus quality to the context and feeling. In the dream, I was not upset, but I was confused with the whole scene. So what did it mean, I asked my therapist-friend. While he didn't "give" me the answer, he suggested that one school of interpretation suggests that the figures we see in our dreams can only be understood as mirror-images of ourselves. So, for example, the place to start in this dream is with the clown; the clown is me, or a part of me, that part of me that goes unrecognized and ignored, if not forgotten. To probe that image for a while—the image of minister as clown, the minister as performer, church as carnival, and how I feel as a participant in all of this— could produce some valuable insights, but only if I'm honest with myself about how I really feel and think about these images.

Carl Jung might have referred to these dream figures as my "shadow," the unaccepted (and unacceptable) parts of my self; those parts of me that I would just as soon never know are there. Indeed, so strong is my desire to believe that these don't exist that one of the only ways I know about them is through my dreams, or by way of some other out-of-the-ordinary type of behavior.

A colleague was telling me about one such experience. A friend of hers called and suggested they go to the mall on a day off. While there, they passed one of these studios where the photographers "make you up" and then take pictures of you. After a great deal of coaxing—which I'm sure included being told that none of her church members would see her or ever know about it—she consented. This was very unlike her, she explained, she doesn't do this kind of thing. They applied "tons of Hollywood makeup" she told me, "and then they do these unimaginable things to your hair and the rest of you. And the dress they *made* me wear," she told me with glee in her voice, "it was simply awful!" And as she walked to the camera, she passed a mirror, and she said she actually startled herself: "Oh my God," she thought, "look at me: that's not me."

It could have been her New England Puritan upbringing, the small-town ethic instilled in her, the culture's image of appropriate ministerial behavior, messages from school, the movies, and books, and probably a combination of all of these and more—they all helped to contribute to her "shadow" side, the part of her self that said dressing and looking "that" way was not her, it was unacceptable. And more: it was bad, it was the demon in her.

As Paul explained to the Corinthians, living is composed of more than those things that make sense, there is much more to living than the appearances that fit our prefab society-, family-, and church-approved images and roles. Yes, there are polarities and life sure would be easy if we fell into one extreme or the other—easy and quite dull. But life is movement and is lived on the continuum that runs between and beyond polarities.

Joel Kovel, in *History and Spirit,* talks about the unaccepted part of self, the shadow, as the "other." Otherness is a function of alienation, he says; the other is the stranger. As you might imagine, otherness has far-reaching implications. If you are interested in understanding how the concept of "shadow" and "other" relate to international and cross-cultural relations, I encourage you to look at Sam Keen's book *Faces of the Enemy: Reflections of the Hostile Imagination.* Here, Keen goes to great lengths to describe and document, in part through propaganda artwork, how the stranger and alien become demonized. He gives some bold and challenging insights into how anyone from governments to churches can play on people's shadow-side fears and thereby nurture and even celebrate the demise of those declared as "different" or demon.

Our loves and hates, fears and hopes, are merely points on a continuum, rather than a scale that demands either/or, and this continuum is a line that allows for the movement of life and behavior. This is what I meant when I said that there's not really a choice other than recognizing that there is no such thing as "not-me," there is only "me," all of me. And me includes the shadow, the other, the stranger.

Our shadow is always there. The harder we might try to ignore it, the more effort we place in denying the demonized in us, the more frightening might our dreams become, the more inappropriate our behavior, the more borderline our fantasies. Given the shadow recognition, accepting it as a part of self, embracing the "other" not as alien or bad, but as different and maybe even of value—this all can be a step toward wholeness.

There is power, confidence, and reconciliation—a kind of atonement—to be found in drawing on your shadow to receive the complete picture of self. Our shadow is neither in the exclusive domain of our dreams or in the reality of everyday life. It is beyond us in the sense that there are probably areas of our self that we will never know. But it is also in a combination achieved by making the unconscious conscious, of becoming deliberate in our attempt to understand ourselves better and to know what it is that makes us think, believe, and behave as we do.

If one of the goals of religion, any religion, is to help the believer achieve wholeness, completeness, atonement, and a sense of peace and being with oneself and the world, then we had better listen to what our demons are saying. The radical commandment given to us by all the world's major religions, to love thy enemy, stranger, neighbor, or foreigner, to love or treat them as yourself, is the way toward both self-knowledge and peace. It is a way to self-understanding that can translate into newer, deeper, more authentic relationships as well as an opportunity to embrace a faith that touches your whole self and spirit.

Easter

Without the Easter story of resurrection—Jesus being raised from the dead—Christianity would not be what it is today. The resurrection story is the quintessential message of Christianity. Yet it is a difficult message—I mean, how can we believe in someone dying on a cross, being placed in a tomb, then coming back to life?

One of the challenges of Easter is moving people to think beyond the Easter event as it's portrayed in the Christian Gospels. I'm not suggesting that we lose the story, but rather that there's more to it than just the story. It's a "mask," the mask of Easter, which is to say that some things aren't what they appear to be. In order to really understand something—a person, an event, a message—you have to remove the mask and look at the larger picture.

I have at home a spirit mask that was carved by a tribesman in New Guinea. It was the custom of his people that when a family member or friend died they would carve an image for the person's spirit. This mask symbolizes not just the dead person, but it points to the past, the present, and the future. It symbolizes the past: the person who once lived. It symbolizes the present: the way that person was brought to life among the people. It symbolizes the future: how the living will be shaped by the continuing presence of the person who has died. So, the mask is more than just the image. It's a symbol.

So it is with the resurrection story. Jesus' life is like a mask, a symbol. It symbolizes the past: the Jesus story is one of transformative hope. It symbolizes the present: his life and teachings become a building block for a creative life. And it symbolizes the future: the lessons he taught can re-birth us when we're stuck, resurrect us when we feel stagnant.

Religion is full of masks—sometimes they come as carved images, or maybe they're from nature, sometimes they are stories that fill us with wonder. We can dwell on the masks themselves or remove them and take the wider view. At Easter, don't get stuck in the obvious: remove the Easter mask; resurrect yourself by looking beyond the obvious.

Epiphany

Religion is a response to the sacred, to what we see and experience as holy. Everyone, I would suggest, experiences something as sacred. It doesn't make any difference who we are, where we are living, what culture informs us—we share common perceptions of the sacred, of those things in life that are experienced to which the only appropriate response is some version of "Wow!" Religion is born when we see the wonder in life—when living is breathtaking, moving, startling. And our response is "Wow!" which when cast in the language of religious dogma or creed can be translated into a variety of words, symbols, rituals, and holidays, including epiphany. An epiphany is an unexpected blessing, gift, insight, or revelation, often of such clarity or profundity that its source feels otherworldly. But it's all simply a version of, a reaction to, "Wow!"

These reactions, these personal epiphanies, might prompt doubt, humility, fear, praise, or uncontrollable joy. These have all been part of the "Wow" experience, our response to the sacred or holy. But to suggest that there is one appropriate response, or one "official" way to respond, without which you are not being religious, assists in giving religion and church bad names. This is not safeguarding our response to the sacred, our response to epiphany.

Life holds epiphanies. While religion is life, it's easy to get stuck: how many times we get stuck in a rut and nearly give up trying to make a new way, simply because of the traditions that keep us in our groove. "It's always been this way," or "What would a newcomer know?" or "If we do it that way, the church may change" (and I'm sure you could add some of your own favorites)—these all are responses to being stuck. They affirm staying stuck! These are not religious responses. When you've been stuck, it can be hard to see the sacred, to experience an epiphany. But it's there, right in front of us, every day. Listen to this story:

A young man became obsessed with a passion for Truth, so he took leave of his family and friends and set out in search of it. He traveled over many lands, sailed across many oceans, climbed many mountains, and all in all, went through a great deal of hardship and suffering.

One day he awoke to find he was seventy-five years old and had still not found the Truth he had been searching for. So he decided, sadly, to give up the search and go back home.

It took him months to return to his homestead, for he was an old man now. Once home, he opened the door of his house—and there he found that Truth had been patiently waiting for him all those years.

The young man turned old man was looking for religion, religious Truth—he was looking for the "Wow!" that would make sense of his life, an epiphany. Did his journeying help him to find it? No, but it prepared him to recognize it. Our life at church can do the same. It can prepare us to name our Truth, to share our response, be it joy, humility, praise, or doubt, when we open our door to home and standing before the sacred we are prompted to say, "Wow!"

Evangelism

John Morgan writes in *Salted with Fire:* "Evangelism is sharing our dream with others in order to transform the world." This isn't a sectarian or denominational idea—it appeals and applies to any person of faith. Defined like this, with the emphasis on sharing faith and not pushing dogma, the issues and questions then become: Do we have a dream worth sharing? Is it a dream with transformative power? If it isn't, then why do we go to church? And if it is, then why do we hold back from sharing it—why isn't it shared so it might transform lives?

Looked at in this way, the sharing of our dream—a form of Unitarian Universalist evangelism—takes on a feel far different than anything we have ever seen or felt. Christian fundamentalist supporters just assume that people want to hear and be a part of their transforming message and movement. It's in this light that religious liberals make a monumental blunder. Adults as well as children will hear about religion—about salvation and sin, grace and blessing, atonement and healing, unitarianism and trinitarianism, evil and goodness. Adults and children will hear these messages from someone. Adults will also hear about the future of a nation welcoming and growing with immigrants, a nation blossoming with religious pluralism and multiculturalism, with communities teeming with diversity. They can hear these messages as proclaimed by the religious Right and Christian fundamentalism, or they can hear these messages from us.

.

Either way adults will hear the message, but who will they hear it from, which version will they get?

For a long time, because of our unwillingness to evangelize—that is to say, to share the transformative power and energy of our faith dreams—adults have been hearing a very lopsided perspective over radio and television, in the print media, and from relatives and neighbors. The alarmist, divisive, exclusivist, punitive, and oppressive dogmatic and creed-filled message of the Christian Right has been loud and strong. But we cannot let it rest there. It's time to transform our communities with the power and energy of our faith dreams. It's time to evangelize!

Evil

I recently took a small, informal poll. "What do you think of evil?" I asked people. Among the responses were laughter, blank stares, comments like "I don't believe in it," "Just what do you mean by evil?" "I'd have to think about it," as well as a few sophisticated answers which included the person who reminded me that "It was said of Mae West that whenever she was forced to choose between two evils, she always picked the one she hadn't tried yet, and would we had the wisdom to do likewise." Among those who wanted to talk about evil, among those who explained what they meant by the word, the distinction was drawn between "bad" and "evil." The difference focuses on intention, deliberateness, personalization. For example, the destruction caused by a hurricane, forest fires, or virus-bearing insects is bad—not deliberate or intended to hurt one person, group or region; there's nothing personal involved; most will agree that these are simply random acts of nature. It would be wrong to call these evil. On the other hand, the ethnic cleansing by Serb leaders, the murders committed by Columbine students, the bombing at Oklahoma City, the torture committed by the Pinochet regime in Chile—these are called evil, bad and evil acts because they were destructive and painful; they hurt people in ways that were not only intentional but out of the ordinary, unreasonable, beyond justification, and outside the scope of human decency and respect. I'm sure you could add to a list of the differences between bad and evil, but in general I think that the differences are marked by intention, deliberateness, and personalization.

But there's more. While no one I've talked with wanted to say much about it, evil seems to carry a deeper sense beyond what I've just described. The qualities of being sinister, insidious, and malevolent take the personal aspect of evil one step further—evil, some suggest, has to do with the character of the person, not just in the act they've committed. That is to say, evil describes more than action and behavior; it's descriptive of the person who does the act, makes the wish, or makes the suggestion: the person is evil.

I'm not talking about "why bad things happen to good people." Nor am I talking about why good things happen to bad people. At this point in my life I'm comfortable with simply answering each with, "Because that's the way things are." But evil, this is different, or at least it feels different. As we were talking about it in a class I teach, I want to affirm and promote the inherent worth and dignity of all people; I want to affirm and promote justice, equity, and compassion in human relations. But where in these two (and in the other five Principles of Unitarian Universalism) do I come to grips with evil? What is it and where does it come from? Let me offer eight explanations, many of which you've heard and perhaps believe.

One theory explains that evil acts are committed by those who suffered early traumatic conditioning that shaped thinking and behavior in powerful and sustaining ways. Another theory explains that evil is dependent on heredity—some kind of an imbalance somewhere in the vast system that makes us tick can throw our whole being out of whack. A third explanation recognizes the importance of the first two but adds that both are subject to the real-life experiences of peer pressure from one's social group. The expectations, lessons, and demands made by your friends and colleagues, whether real or perceived as real, are significant in determining behavior. Fourth, the choice factor: it's your choice as to how you want to act, it's called free will, you can do whatever you like, right or wrong, good or evil. Regardless of what happened growing up, no matter what you've inherited, it makes no difference who your friends are, you know what's right and what's wrong and you can choose, and then deal with the consequences determined by your choice.

Next, even if all of these four are accurate and even truthful explanations for why evil is done, the fifth explanation says that it was karma that made it so; it has happened this way because of something from the past, a past life, and though we don't understand why it's exactly happening this way, we can be sure that there is an overall plan, a cosmic pattern of which we are just a small part. A sixth theory: something essentially human is missing; there's a piece missing from the character inventory—as if to say, evil is committed not because of something but because of the lack of something decidedly human. Then there are two more explanations with which I want to spend a little more time because of the importance I think they have—they are among the most common reasons given for the existence and recognition of evil.

Let me tell you about an experience to get to the first one. One of the few outstanding recollections I have from elementary school is of one afternoon on the playground during recess. It's a moving snapshot: a good friend, Steve, is pinned against a chain-link fence with his stomach and face turned away from the crowd of kids who are stoning him with fistfuls of gravel while shouting in unison, "Jew-boy, Jew-boy, Jew-boy." I don't know why it happened, I don't remember how it ended. But I can still see it and hear them. I must have eventually gone to someone for an explanation—a teacher, my minister, a neighbor, it could have been my Wednesday lunchtime Bible school instructor—someone told me that Christians hold Jews responsible for the death of Jesus Christ, the Son of God, and that could have been the reason for the stoning. It was said almost as if this was a plausible and justifiable reason.

Poor Steve seemed to be bearing the brunt of some people's decision to blame Jesus' death on Jews and the eventual demonization of Jews by some Christians (and then if you want to play it all the way out you'd have to include the demonization of Jews and Christians by some Muslims). Yet this whole process is a superb and enlightening (and often entertaining) piece of the history of how evil came from nowhere into somewhere, and continues to be lived out in examples like the Southern Baptist Convention's proselytizing of Jews on Yom Kippur.

Evil and western religious belief have been intertwined for at least three millennia. To say that it is a thread in our cultural fabric would be a profound understatement—it covers us, we can't get away from it, it's everywhere: it's in the novels we read, the fairy tales we tell, the shows we watch; it's in the classroom, the newspaper, descriptions of athletic events; it's in our dreams, fantasies, myths, and conversations over coffee. The forces of righteousness versus Satan, the children of light and dark, the sons and daughters of Cain and Abel, the Empire versus the Rebellion. It's everywhere: good versus evil. This is as integral and essential to Western heritage as anything. It's who we are, it is the way we have been taught to think and to feel. So this, then, is a seventh explanation for evil: there are demons out there, people and spirits who are intent on doing us harm, who are agents of the demonic, of Evil (with a capital "E").

And finally the eighth explanation: we create evil. Of course bad people exist, of course evil things are done to the innocent, without a doubt acts of evil alarm us all. And we create evil. Listen to Sam Keen: "Generation after generation, we find excuses to hate and dehumanize each other, and we always justify ourselves with the most mature-sounding political rhetoric. And we refuse to admit the obvious. We human beings are *Homo hostilis,* the hostile species, the enemy-making animal. We are driven to fabricate an enemy. From the unconscious residue of our hostility, we create a target; from our private demons, we conjure a public enemy." (*Faces of the Enemy*) The creation of Jews as the enemy of some Christians, the belief that Jews and Christians are the enemies of some Muslims, suggest Keen and others, these enemies and evildoers are not empirical fact, but psychological fact. They are projections of group denial, of things that members of the group won't acknowledge about themselves.

Keen is talking about the shadow, an idea discussed by Swiss psychiatrist Carl Jung but recognized as truth in Eastern religions before there was a Jesus. For everything we see about ourselves and others, there's a hidden side, a shadow side. Evil can be explained as the projections of our shadow side. Health according to Jung, spiritual completeness according to Hinduism and Buddhism, is recognizing and knowing that we are whole, not just unconscious shadow or conscious self, but both together, yin and yang (as in Taoism). Demons will always exist until this completeness is achieved. The denial and lack of attention to your shadow side, then, is the eighth and final explanation for evil.

Regardless of where you are in the shaping of your thoughts about these, include these thoughts from Aleksandr Solzhenitsyn: "If only it were all so simple! If only there were evil people somewhere insidiously committing evil deeds, and it were necessary only to separate them from the rest of us and destroy them. But the line dividing good and evil cuts through the heart of every human being. And who is willing to destroy a piece of his own heart?"

Keeping your heart whole means coming to terms with your whole self, with those ideas, beliefs, and fears that you project out onto other people and groups. As I said earlier, it's so easy to dismiss evil by thinking of it as merely a matter of projection: there is evil in the world, there is a lot of needless suffering that is caused by evil acts that should not go unpunished. It's very easy to create an enemy and say they're at fault. But the results of separation and blaming are racism and genocide, ethnic cleansing and school murders, hate crimes and conspiracy bombings. Point the finger everywhere but at ourselves? No. As Solzhenitsyn so eloquently puts it, we are all one and inseparable. Therefore, let us choose our language carefully and honestly, speaking truth to power with humility.

Faith

Like many of the issues and questions raised in religious circles nowadays, a great deal of the challenge in talking about faith revolves around definition. What does it mean to have faith, to be a person of faith? Believers and followers toss this word around as though there is a commonly understood definition—and up to a point there is.

We might all agree with this: that religious faith refers to a set of beliefs or principles. For some, these beliefs are defined by the experiences, history, teachings, and authority of those who claim loyalty to a particular religious way. When you ask them if they have faith and they say yes, what they often mean is that they have faith in belief, that is, they support and believe the faith as taught by their religious way, which if institutionalized will come fully equipped with books and creeds and dogma and hierarchy, "smells and bells," and all those things that are supposed to make faith easier for them as a follower.

This is one form of faith—faith as belief. According to my biblical thesaurus, the one who has faith: *is blessed* (Ps. 40:4; 84:12; Prov. 16:20; Jer. 17:7); *will never thirst* (John 6:35); *is radiant* (Ps. 34:5); *is delivered* (Ps. 22:4); *is like Mount Zion* (Ps. 125:1); *will not be moved* (Isa. 28:16; 1 Pet. 2:6); *will not be disappointed* (Rom. 9:33; 10:11); *has prayers heard* (1 Chron. 5:20); *will prosper* (Prov. 28:25); *will be safe* (Prov. 29:25); *is surrounded by loving-kindness* (Ps. 32:10); *is kept in perfect peace* (Isa. 26:3); *has rivers of living water flowing from him* (John 7:38); *does not remain in darkness* (John 12:46). My goodness! For all of that, who wouldn't want faith? Yes, the promises of faith have been many—just turn on your radio and TV and listen to the promises of faith. Just believe (and occasionally send in some money)—JUST BELIEVE—have faith, and you will be rewarded, we're told. Faith as belief, as suggested by many, means a faith in spite of evidence; faith as acceptance of the hard-to-believe; faith as blind obedience to authority.

I'm sure you have known, heard about, experienced those whose faith is a crutch, a shield, a wall that keeps them hidden and protected from people, issues, and realities that they would prefer not to deal with. I know those, and perhaps you do too, who need this kind of faith in belief, for it might be all that stands between them and physical, emotional, or spiritual breakdown. What I'm suggesting is that sometimes the call is a close one; sometimes it does seem appropriate to support a belief in "whatever gets you through the night."

You have probably heard the expression, "It's not good enough to just talk the walk; you've got to walk your talk." Some would suggest that this is analogous to faith—there's faith as talk, that is belief; then there's faith as walk, that is behavior. There are those who have failed to make the connection between their behavior and their faith—it's as though the two have nothing to do with each other: over here is what they believe, and over there is how they behave. Faith and behavior appear to have no relationship. And then there are those who seem to act all the time, but don't appear to have faith in much; they are all doing and no being, all walking and no talking. From the way they live, it appears they've never given much thought to grounding themselves in faith, or at least they have not thought through why they live the way they do.

Faith as behavior, like faith as belief, has strong biblical roots. In the letter of James, he makes a strong argument supporting faith as works, a tradition that both

Unitarians and Universalists referred to as "deeds not creeds." In James 2:14–18 it says:

> What good is it my brothers and sisters, if you say you have faith but do not have works? Can faith save you? If a brother or sister is naked and lacks daily food, and one of you says to them: "Go in peace. Keep warm and eat your fill," and yet you do not supply their bodily needs, what is the good of that? So faith by itself, if it has no works, is dead. . . .
> Show me your faith apart from your works, and I by my works will show you my faith.

What this suggests is that faith as belief and faith as behavior (as works) together comprise faith—neither can stand alone, for alone they are but a fraction of faith, but never complete.

Allan Jones defines faith like this: "Faith is the willingness to have one's story tested by a larger narrative that one takes on trust." (*The Soul's Journey*) I think this means that we each have our story. It's composed of all the events and transitions, all the people and pets, all the loves and hates, all the everything that is our life experience. When we bring this story, the story of our lives, into the context and perspective of a larger story/narrative called a religious tradition, we let that tradition speak to us to see if it fits, if it makes order of our story, if it gives our story roots and wings, stability and ecstasy, explanation and spirit, sense and mystery. We do this willingly, with faith, and if that tradition—the narrative—affirms us in who we are, in our story, then we choose, convert, or follow that religious tradition: it has gained our allegiance, our trust. And so, a third form of faith: faith as trust.

You can see then, that faith is a complex subject with many dimensions and levels. Don't be too eager to embrace too much or dismiss the obvious or the hard-to-understand. We all have faith, and deciphering what it is and how we arrived at it is an exploration well worth the effort.

Family Values

Imagine that all around you—among your relatives, neighbors, coworkers, parents of your children's friends, in the volunteer organizations you serve, in the exercise class you attend—imagine that conservative and fundamentalist religious persons are saying that the nation and our communities are deteriorating because there's no support for "family values" (which has been code language for religious values, i.e., Christian values). Just imagine. How will you respond when asked to defend your silence: "Where do you go to church?" someone may ask you. "What do you believe? What are your church's 'family values'?"

All of these questions, contexts, and circumstances are not easy—not for any of us. And for the church-attending person, for the person who takes their spiritual and religious life seriously, these are questions and issues that we cannot avoid or walk quietly around. It's questions and issues of this sort that have, at least in part, brought many to Unitarian Universalism.

So, imagine telling someone unfamiliar with Unitarian Universalism, "I go to the Unitarian Universalist Church where I have 'an opportunity to pursue ultimate religious questions within a context which respects mystery and is open to a multitude of revelations.'" Imagine telling this to someone who has never known anything but a more conservative, orthodox, even fundamentalist religious tradition. You might as well be speaking a different language. Frankly, I don't even try to have this conversation anymore. Yet, it is a conversation that you will have the opportunity to have. Especially as the nation seems to become more focused on questions and issues of morality, ethics, and order, the role and meaning of religious values, or "family values," becomes more and more central. So here are some words of guidance regarding what our Unitarian Universalist faith holds up as being of religious and spiritual value—for you will be asked, you will want to know.

I suggest these three values, values that are woven together so finely that to tug on one pulls on another: personal *authenticity,* religious *honesty,* and human *community.* Authenticity, honesty, and community are three values, "family" values if you like, that we as Unitarian Universalists, as adults, youth, and children, embrace in our religious faith, regardless of where we go—our neighborhoods, as citizens of our nation, as members of the world.

Harold Kushner tells of visiting an Episcopalian priest who is in the last stages of dying. He has AIDS and wonders if his congregation will take him back, if they will accept him as he is, for who he is. He wants to go back, if only to give one more sermon: "'I have to share with them the lesson my illness has taught me,'" he tells Kushner. "'You don't have to be perfect. Just do your best, and God will accept you as you are. Don't expect your children to be perfect. Love them for their trying and stumbling.'" (*How Good Do We Have to Be*) I believe he is talking about an authentic life.

Accepting people for who they are—not who they would/could/should be; accepting people where they are, not where we think they ought to be; accepting people for what they are, not as we would like them; to be the best we can be, that is perfection, that is authenticity—perfection is authenticity. Isn't authenticity all that any parent, friend, or lover really wishes for their child, friend, or mate? Of course, there's a lot that gets in the way, along the way: family, work, friends, the media, and religion—it can feel as though all these are conspiring to push us in directions we really don't want to go. So look deeper, ask the soul-searching questions and I think you'll find that it's personal authenticity that is the real perfection. Just be the best you can be. What more can we ask of another or of ourselves, than to strive for, embrace, and share an authentic life?

Personal authenticity, then, is a value that we as Unitarian Universalists affirm. And it very neatly creates the setting for a second value essential to and encouraged by our faith: religious honesty, especially as reflected in religious thoughtfulness and integrity. We simply ask that as Unitarian Universalists you be honest about your beliefs and about the process that you use in arriving at your faith, and that you be honest about where you are on your faith journey. For us, religious faith is not about who gets there first or how quickly you get to wherever you're going, it's not about how long you've been there or even how few U-turns and detours you took. Religious honesty, thoughtfulness, and integrity are what we affirm.

There can be misunderstanding about doubt (which is the perception of struggling with faith), that doubt in a religious context is a negative thing. In Unitarian Universalism, doubt and faith have coexisted, even thrived, for centuries. Doubt has never been a problem because we understand that the opposite of faith is not doubt, but despair. And if there is one thing that Unitarian Universalism has always affirmed, for nearly 500 years, it is the promise of faith in spite of the possibility of despair! As Unitarian Universalists, we affirm the value of religious honesty—honesty in a faith context—which might mean doubt, but never means a lack of hope, never a lack of faith.

Building on the religious values of personal authenticity and religious honesty, a third Unitarian Universalist family value to share with others is the value of human community. We live in very scary times. We all have every right to be edgy, a bit anxious about what might happen next. The desire for certainty, often viewed as the wish for security, is strong: just to know that everything is going to be okay, that we are ultimately on solid footing, that while we may slide a bit, we won't go too far—is this too much to ask for?

Some turn to religion for security, seeking stability in the certitude of creeds, commandments, and catechisms. This quest for certainty, according to some, is the reason why conservative and fundamentalist religions everywhere have swelled their ranks to historical numbers and why moderate and liberal religions have been losing membership in record-breaking ways. But there's always an exception to these kinds of trends, and one sociologist of religion puts it this way: "One may observe in passing that an interesting bit of 'anti-[certainty]' data comes from the robust growth of the Unitarian Universalist church in recent years—a community that can hardly be called 'strong' [in its quest for certainty]." (Peter Berger in *The Christian Century*)

It's not that we embrace insecurity or instability; it's that we affirm and promote principles and values that others, chief among them the fundamentalist and conservative faiths, think lead to and strengthen uncertainty. For example, the first two of our principles, "We affirm and promote the inherent worth and dignity of every person; we affirm and promote justice, equity and compassion," are religious principles in our way of faith. We place great value on incorporating these into our faith and living by them. Affirming and promoting the inherent worth and dignity of every person by promoting justice, equity, and compassion are family values that we encourage all our members and friends to pursue and live.

We abhor the uncertainty and insecurity that many, who because of their gender, ethnicity, ableness, age, or sexual orientation, must live with due to the certainty that many consider them "inferior" and will discriminate against them if given the opportunity. We abhor the uncertainty and insecurity that many risk when they choose to be authentic and religiously honest about who they are and what they believe. We abhor the uncertainty and insecurity that results from the fear of different ideas, customs, beliefs, and backgrounds. We believe that the only way to find lasting certainty and security is with an affirmation of the human community as our community—not by cutting away, denying, or oppressing what we disagree with or what's different from us.

We "affirm and promote respect for the interdependent web of all existence," and that means we value the human community, of which we are a part. Appreciation and respect for the whole human community is a Unitarian Universalist family value.

We embrace and hold up authenticity, honesty, and community as essential in our liberal religious faith. What is most critical and instrumental for us is that these family values are not just something to talk about during our time together; they are not merely something that we teach and talk about in the church school; authenticity, honesty, and community aren't just social justice projects that we take on periodically. These are values of faith, to be lived out now, among each other, in our neighborhoods, and in the larger community.

Flesh (John 1:14)

Why is the church involved in speaking to and about sexuality issues? What's it got to do with religion and church?

It's because "The Word became flesh," as stated in John 1:14. We didn't ask for it that way, it just is. Now of course, one interpretation of this passage—the narrower and more restrictive one—is that the Word was with God and the Word, that is God, became, through Jesus, flesh, human, one of us, on earth, which is all to say God came to earth. In a broader way, "The Word became flesh" simply means that the mystery which some call holy is among us, is *in* us; this mystery called God is as close to us as is the flesh on our bodies. Our flesh—our "skin"—is holy. We cannot separate our sexuality from our spirituality—talk about the "interdependent web" of which we are all a part—this is it at its most intimate level: "The Word became flesh."

This is why sexuality issues are so difficult: it's because all issues of sexuality are rhetorical, they end up being questions, challenges, and issues about our selves, about our own sexuality and spirituality. This was assured when the Word became flesh—there's no running or hiding from it, and there's no successful denial either. Our sexuality, as with our spirituality, is intrinsic to who we are, it is our essence. And because we know all of this— maybe it's hard to acknowledge and we all acknowledge it in a different ways, but we do know it—we are vulnerable in ways that make some tremble and shudder as at no other time. How and to whom will I be vulnerable?

Vulnerability is a significant if not determining variable when it comes to addressing sexuality issues.

Many are unable to see through the haze because the messages we've received from family, peers, church, and society are so mixed, confused, and conflicting. Due to this, I often think think that anyone who can think and see with clarity is amazing. I was really struck with the way Sam Keen expresses this:

> As sex rears its marvelous-awful head, we reach the opalescent heart of confusion. No human activity is so surrounded with glory and baseness, so full of divine promise and demonic power. It may be the ultimate sacrament, the spiritual union of lovers, god and goddess, and yang and yin, or it may be the degraded humping of anonymous bodies. It may be a path that leads to beatific union or to pandemonium. Whatever else we may say about sexuality, we must begin by acknowledging that it is surrounded by a cloud of obsessions, a thorn thicket of guilt, a swamp of shame, a double wall of dogma and taboo, and several veils of romantic illusion. We approach it knowing we are at best one-eyed and at worst blind and must grope our way carefully through the haze. (*Hymns to an Unknown God*)

At least some of the confusion is the result of misunderstanding as well as ignorance. Sexuality refers to a broad range of issues and challenges about our bodies and relationships, about knowledge and intimacy, about biology and physiology, about gender and gender roles, lovemaking and dating, about values and sexual orientation, about abuse, harassment, and rape. These are all sexuality issues.

It's too bad that our culture has convinced so many that any time the word s-e-x appears in whatever form, it means one thing only: the sexual act, intercourse, making love. In allowing this to happen, in limiting it to this level of thinking, sexuality is debased by those who are often the ones complaining about its debasing. They turn human sexuality (and spirituality) into one word and one act. Is this not a form of idolatry?

"The Word became flesh" is a beautiful reality. All we have to do is look at each other to understand its beauty and depth.

Forgiveness

In a favorite prayer of mine, Harry Meserve writes:

> From arrogance, pompousness, and from thinking ourselves more important than we are, may some saving sense of humor liberate us. For allowing ourselves to ridicule the faith of others, may we be forgiven.
>
> For making war and calling it peace, special privilege and calling it justice, indifference and calling it tolerance, pollution and calling it progress, may we be cured.
>
> For telling ourselves and others that evil is inevitable while good is impossible, may we stand corrected.
>
> God of our mixed up, tragic, aspiring, doubting and insurgent lives, help us to be as good as in our hearts we have always wanted to be. Amen. (found in *Singing the Living Tradition*)

How do we respond to the words and thoughts that well up in us after reading this? As you read Meserve's words, perhaps you recalled individuals or contexts that came to mind earlier today or this week. When we are challenged, confronted, or feeling victimized, when accused, abused, or misused, we have at least three ways to respond: avoidance, resentment, or forgiveness.

It seems to me that the first two, avoidance and resentment, come so laden with possible danger and harm that it's the equivalent to a lifetime of walking through minefields: you know the potential for explosion is imminent, but you're not totally sure when it will happen. It has been my experience, personally and from observation, that many choose to stay with resentment and avoidance simply because they feel like there's less effort required. Like a familiarity with land that has been mined, though buried with life-altering dangers that might remain submerged long past the conflict, familiar responses do have a security about them, unlike the open and honest, but perhaps painfully discomforting, process of forgiveness. And while resentment and avoidance which remain buried for a lifetime may surface and explode, destroying or maiming at the slightest vibration, forgiveness promotes dialogue, understanding, healing, and wholeness.

Forgiveness is no easy thing: it involves turning, and turning means effort and resolve. It means intention and direction. Forgiveness could mean, as Lewis Smedes puts it, "surrender[ing] the right to get even because forgiving is always a decision to put up with an uneven score." (*Context*)

There are four components to forgiveness: remorse, resolution, restitution, and restoration. Remorse is what most are familiar with, in fact some consider it synonymous with forgiveness. Remorse means being genuinely sorry for what has happened. Of course, it's not just a matter of saying the words; remorse is not social etiquette or duty, it's not excusing oneself, it's not good manners or something you learn along the way. Remorse is not taught as you might learn math or Spanish—there are no formulas or tricks to getting it right. Remorse is genuinely felt. "I'm sorry, forgive me" aren't simply convenient words that act as a transition back to the routine. Remorse is rooted in the strong, sincere, and deeply felt awareness that someone has been hurt.

Next is resolution, the determination to change, to not repeat whatever it was that caused the hurt. This isn't always such a simple thing, and I think it's sometimes made too easy—let's call it asking for cheap forgiveness. I have a colleague who was telling me about a man in his congregation who was in the hospital dying. Just days before his death, he told his wife that he'd had several affairs during their thirty-year marriage—he said he didn't want to die without getting it off his chest, asking her for forgiveness. In choosing to tell his wife about these affairs, at the last minute, this man was continuing his self-serving, thoughtless behavior—he was asking for cheap forgiveness because there was no opportunity for him to show how he was going to change, to show that he meant what he said, there was no chance for resolution. The man's wife was so angry, she felt so used, that she walked out of the room and didn't come back until after he'd died.

After remorse and resolution, there's restitution, which means the chance to rebuild and live a new life, the opportunity to start over. I remember hearing the story of a young high school age woman who had been raised by a father who abused her sexually. She knew it was wrong but was always terrified to say anything. Even after his death, when she was in college, she was afraid. Finally, with the support of her therapist, she told the rest of her family. They were stunned, but didn't know what to do to bring closure and restitution. Without even asking, the father's brother, the woman's uncle, flew in to see her. He apologized to her for his brother's abuse and violation and promised her that he would do everything he could to help her start again, to rebuild her life, to put as many of the pieces back into a whole as possible.

Restitution, this rebuilding process, is the desire to make things whole again. And while this might have to take a long time, still the need for atonement is crucial, it's crucial for all of us, it's an integral piece of the forgiving process. The need for wholeness, for restitution, is a part of the forgiving process. Rebuilding is as important as the other components of forgiveness.

Finally, there's restoration, reintegration into one's community, the desire for relationship. Following the brutalization of his son in the hands of a local police officer, Lewis Smedes wrote:

> I'm not very good at spiritual disciplines; but after being told to practice what I preach by a friend, I sat alone in

my study and made believe I was a priest in a confessional. I said out loud, "Officer, in the name of God, I forgive you." I felt the caricature I had made of the officer begin to change . . . interestingly, a year later the same cop drove past our house and I had to go through the whole forgiveness process all over again. . . . Forgiving by fallible creatures is repetitious.

Entering back into relationship after a person has been wronged doesn't come easily. To say that we're simply human is stating the obvious—we can be thoughtless or mean, or we might even think what we were doing was right. But eventually, the need for healing will rise to the surface. In his desire to enter back into relationship, listen to these words of remorse and restoration spoken by a former South African soldier in his testimony in front of families he'd attacked in a rural village, as reported in *The Christian Century*. Facing his victims he said: "I can never undo what I have done. I have no right to ask your forgiveness, but I ask that you will allow me to spend my life helping you to rebuild your village and put your lives together."

Remorse, resolution, restitution, and restoration— this is the process of forgiveness. As you think about this possibility, as you reflect on these thoughts, consider some additional words from Reinhold Niebuhr:

> Nothing that is worth doing can be achieved in our lifetime; therefore we must be saved by hope. Nothing which is true or beautiful or good makes complete sense in any immediate context of history; therefore we must be saved by faith. Nothing we do, however virtuous, can be accomplished alone; therefore we are saved by love. No virtuous act is quite as virtuous from the standpoint of our friend or foe as it is from our standpoint. Therefore we must be saved by the final form of love, which is forgiveness. (found in *Singing the Living Tradition*)

Free Faith

In the Free Faith called Unitarian Universalism, we place an immense amount of trust (faith) in freedom, the freedom of belief and the way that freedom of belief (freedom from creed and dogma) will in turn shape individual faith. I see this in several aspects of the narrative/story that we identify as our religious way.

First, as the Free Faith we read and appreciate more than one sacred story or tradition. Our Principles and Purposes affirm the many living traditions from which we draw guidance and inspiration. I think many Unitarian Universalists would find humorous yet meaningful a *New Yorker* cartoon that shows a couple sitting, and the woman is saying to the man: "Don't worry honey—the big questions are multiple choice," suggesting that sometimes there's more than one answer—there's *your* answer, *your* faith. Put another way: no religious tradition has the corner on truth. What it has is its version of the truth, its rendition of the story.

Second, and continuing with this line of thinking, as the Free Faith we are not only trusting of our tradition, but trusting of others: I believe that Unitarian Universalism is a bold, enthusiastic, and progressive step forward toward open and free religious thinking. Alan Jones writes that he has a friend who "claims that people have either a fortress or a banquet mentality. They see everything in terms of either defense and protection or sharing and celebration." For me, our Free Faith has always symbolized a banquet table at which no creed or dogma was the price of welcome.

Third: many religious traditions carry within them stories of miracles. Often central to faith is the unbelievable occurring and belief in these miraculous events; faith is trusting in these stories of miracles. I think that many of the followers of our Free Faith also believe in miracles. I know that our Free Faith has been called by some a rational religion, so you may wonder how a rational religion can affirm miracles. Listen to this: When *New York Times* religion writer Ari Goldman took his sabbatical at Harvard Divinity School and later published his experiences in the book *The Search for God at Harvard,* he included this story, an experience that puts miracles into perspective:

> After class, I walked Jacob home and told him what troubled me. "Once you show that the Torah is flawed, that it is not really God-given, what happens to your faith? What is your Judaism? What compels you to lead a religious life? What is its binding force?"
>
> Jacob listened to me patiently and then pointed to a stately oak ablaze with fall colors. "Do you know how that tree began?" he asked. He bent down and picked up an acorn and rolled it in his fingers. "Just because you know how it began doesn't mean you cannot enjoy the tree."

Every time someone in the congregation has a baby, every time I walk the beach and watch the waves, every time I have the opportunity to share in the love of two people, every time I see or experience the warmth and care of my congregation, every time I look up at the stars on a clear night—although I usually know the whys and hows and whens of those specific moments—still it's amazing, it's fantastic, it is miraculous! The Free Faith doesn't restrict the way I see and interact with my world; the Free Faith affirms me and my world in all its beauty.

These have been just a few of the elements embraced by our Free Faith. Many of them at first glance, by name at least, are the same as in other religions. Miracles, stories, explanations, answers, certainty of faith—these are the essential things of religious conversation and conversion.

If you begin to get the impression that the Free Faith is both deep and wide, it is. Our faith is both rich and profound in its embrace, which is why it's often called the Liberal Faith. For the way of our faith is not one way, but many. If the root meaning of the word *religion* means "to bind," then our way of binding includes many paths, many traditions. We embrace no one specific set of ways that we then call religious, telling our people, "Here, just follow this path, this set of rules, this dogma, just say these creeds."

What it is that we do say is that we are all a part of an interdependent web of life—each one of us—and we are bound up in this web together. The web of life is very complex, intricate, and in many ways both strong and fragile. We each are but one strand in this web, and understanding how we are woven into this web called life is the task of religion. For those of the Free Faith, it would be presumptuous to say there is but one way to be religious because life tells us just the opposite: there are many ways. There is *your* way of religion—and in the Free Faith we share and explore the interdependent web of life while affirming "the inherent worth and dignity of every person."

There are those who fear falling in their religion, who fear falling from the path of faith. They think that religion is restrictive rather than liberating, confining rather than freeing, punitive instead of affirming. The Free Faith embraces us as we are and says there is no need to fear falling from the path because, first, there are many paths to be tried and it's a matter of finding yours, and second, we are part of a strong web which, if you let it, will buoy and support you along your way.

> I leave you with an image from the Wallenda family, [writes colleague Dick Gilbert in a sermon] the Wallenda family of high wire acrobats and artists. Karl Wallenda once said, "Being on the tightrope is living; everything else is waiting." For more than 50 years he walked the tightrope

with grace, but one afternoon, while doing the human pyramid, the Wallendas had an accident. Karl's son was paralyzed and his daughter-in-law was killed. After that nothing was the same. A short time later he too fell to his death. When his wife was asked what had happened, she said, "All his life Karl had walked the tightrope. But for the last few months all he thought about was falling. It was the first time he'd thought about that and it seemed to me he put all his energy into not falling rather than in walking the tightrope."

The Free Faith is not concerned with falling, but with living—with living each day, with getting up every morning and walking whatever path it is we have chosen as our way of being bound to life. For me, for us, the Free Faith as belief, as works, as trust is a glorious, vibrant, and meaningful path to living religiously. Let us sing, dance, and share its melodies as we weave the web of life.

Fundamentalism

I'll often hear some, especially religious liberals, refer to evangelicals and fundamentalists in the same breath. People talk about "evangelical, fundamentalist Christians" all at once, as if everyone understands what this means, as if it all means the same thing. The media is especially fond of lumping these groups together. But there are important distinctions to be made within conservative Protestantism. The largest grouping is born-again Christians, a term that we've heard many times. Born-again Christians comprise the largest number of conservative Christians. Subsets then follow. The first subset is evangelicals, who are born-again and believe in the authority of scripture, as well as in a direct experience with God; they also believe in sharing the Gospel (evangelism). The next subset is fundamentalists who are born-again evangelicals who additionally believe in the inerrancy of scripture, that is, the literal translation of biblical texts. (Other subsets would include Pentecostals, charismatics, and others).

To be a religious fundamentalist means to be anti-modern, it means being opposed to what the modern world not only symbolizes, but what it actually is. And it makes little difference what kind of religious fundamentalist you are—Christian, Islamic, Jewish, Black Muslim—all fundamentalists share an abhorrence for modernity. Without an understanding of this, you will be lost in today's world, a world that is witnessing a growing fundamentalist movement.

Perhaps you've had the experience of listening to a fundamentalist preacher—it makes no difference what religious faith he (and more often than not, it is a man) is espousing—and after a while shaking your head because what you're hearing simply no makes no sense. It's beyond comprehension, as though the message were in another language, as if the person and you were not inhabiting the same earth. My mistake is in assuming that we do speak the same language, that we inhabit the same earth. Harvey Cox has said:

> In the subculture of fundamentalism people talk and think differently. Like any subculture, fundamentalism challenges the dominant culture not so much in its explicit ideas but in its unspoken premises. . . . It is fundamentalism's relative isolation from mainstream theology that enables it to pose questions (albeit in ways that sometimes seem exasperating and even eccentric) no one within the mainstream would think of voicing. (*The Atlantic*)

Very few in the circles most of us live in would ever question the world about us, but this is precisely what the fundamentalist does. The world, the modern world, is not what it should be, it is not what it could be, according to the fundamentalist: the world has gone astray. Rather than participating in it or attempting to reshape it from within, the fundamentalist seeks to remain detached, removed, at a distance, in a subculture—a world of their own which clings to the way life ought to be, which clutches to the fundamentals of the one and only true way. Their objective is to change the world so that their religion will be easier to live: they don't want to translate their message into the world's terms, but bring the world into line with their message.

Now, as a theology, as a way of living with the world, none of this may make any sense to you. On a logical, rational level, many simply can't comprehend this approach. But the lure of fundamentalism isn't in the surface beliefs—it's in what's behind it. It's a very messy world that we live in. We probably all have our moments when we'd just like to chuck it all. I used to have a friend who felt that way. She just wanted to hide out as a potato farmer in northern Maine—until she met me. Having lived in Maine for seven years, I could tell her what I'd observed about life as a potato farmer in northern Maine: it wasn't a great place to hide out from the world. Indeed, they had problems all their own! But the lure of escaping was quite appealing.

The lure of fundamentalism is strong. First, it's dualistic—there's never more than an either/or choice. There's right or wrong, good or bad, the righteous or the sinner. In this sense, everything is very easy to understand, it's all right in front of you—there are two choices for everything. Dualism makes for a lot of security and safety. As a follower of fundamentalism, you're boxed in, and for many that feels very good, especially in a world where their appear to be no limits, no walls, no shoulds or shouldn'ts.

Second, as a follower of fundamentalism, you are always among the correct—you're right and "they" are wrong. And so enters religious anger. John Spong writes in *Rescuing the Bible from Fundamentalism* that if you are among the true believers: " . . . it becomes not merely justifiable but downright righteous to utter words of condemnation and prayers for the early demise of the enemy. Indeed, you can even believe that you are God's anointed one to rid the world of a demonic figure."

But you see, even though these are just a few of the possible lures behind the spoken words of fundamentalism, it goes further still. I'm reminded of the story of a sergeant who was asking a group of recruits why walnut was used for the butt of a rifle. "Because it is harder than other woods," said one man. "Wrong," said the sergeant. "Because it is more elastic." "Wrong again," shouted the sergeant. "Because it has a better shine." "You boys certainly have a lot to learn," complained the sergeant. "Walnut is used for the simple reason that it is laid down in the Regulations."

Fundamentalism is a "regulations" way of faith. As with anything where there is a set of rules, there is little room, perhaps no room, for interpretation. In religious fundamentalism, we see this with holy scripture: both conservatives and fundamentalists (and others) will agree about the authority of scripture, but the fundamentalist holds fast to the inerrancy of it—it is regulations, and what it says, is.

Putting an interesting twist to this, Thomas Moore says that this allows fundamentalism to be "a defense against the overtones of life." You follow the letter of the word, no more, no less, that's it—no interpretation, no metaphors or symbols, no analysis. Consequently, writes Moore, "The tragedy of fundamentalism in any context is its capacity to freeze life into a solid cube of meaning." (*Care of the Soul*)

In this is one of the many ironies in Christian fundamentalism. Many of the early followers of Jesus, especially the disciples, were fundamentalist to the core, which drove Jesus crazy! For example, he was constantly talking to them and others in metaphor and symbol; his parables, for instance, cannot be understood superficially, but only by reading beyond the word, reading in depth. After so many of his teachings he had to sit his disciples down and explain what he meant, explain the overtones, the shaded areas of his message, what wasn't obvious in the words alone. I wonder how much has changed today: Christian fundamentalists continue reading the words of Jesus without understanding the overtones, but taking what he said, as did his disciples, at face value. And it still is driving people crazy!

The danger is that anyone can fall into their own fundamentalism, including religious liberals. The most common way that I see Unitarian Universalists becoming wishful thinkers is when we become as insistent, ardent, and outspoken about being open as the fundamentalist does about being closed. Also, as in few other established mainline religious institutions, New Age thought, in its broadest sense, has caught hold and won a following. New Age, like fundamentalism, shares a certain distrust and protest over the airtight arguments of modernism: rationalism, science, and organization, even the separation of nation-states, are all held at an arm's length. It's these, and more, that both the fundamentalist and the New Ager hold as being responsible for and contributing to the demise of life as it could be. One thing this can lead to is a self-righteousness that is nearly (if not completely) intolerable for the unsuspecting passerby, or whoever happens to be in the path of the believer's piety.

Since the 1500s, Unitarian Universalists have held fast to the principles of freedom, reason, and tolerance, kind of a built-in trinity of belief and practice that for the most part has done us well. These three principles have kept the straightjacket of fundamentalism away from our faith. Unitarian Universalism has never been a religious faith to back away from the world, from the world as it is. Very different from the fundamentalist, our way of faith is one that expects and often demands our full attention and engagement in modern life.

God I

Across the street and on the corner from the church I served in Maine was a gas station. The station owner and I were on friendly speaking terms, though I think I remained somewhat of a mystery to him. I say this based on the monthly conversations we'd have when he happened to be out pumping gas and I walked by on my way to town. Our pattern was always the same: one of us would begin the conversation, which inevitably would turn to a local topic, which would lead to a national or international issue, which would highlight the differences and incongruities of human behavior and lead my gas-pumping, small-town, station-owning theologian to conclude: "Well, at least we all believe in the same God," which meant that the conversation was over and all was right with the world, at least his world. He would turn to walk away leaving me standing there, somewhat mystified and confused by his abruptness if not his conclusion.

I always wanted to yell to him, as he walked into the station office, "But that's just the point—we don't all believe in the same God." So why didn't I? I suppose I was apprehensive that he might say "What?" and then, well, then I'd have to explain the realities of God and God's believers. It's the same reality that those who continue to claim that God is dead have to face. God is very much alive and there is no consensus of who or what this God is—confusion reigns. Several years ago, before the nation's newspaper editors and publishers, Shirley MacLaine shared these sobering thoughts:

Consider this: In the Name of God, a Fatwa against Salman Rushdie. In the Name of God, murder in the Balkans. In the Name of God, the bombing of the World Trade Center in New York. In the Name of God, the Siege at Waco, Texas. In the Name of God, Hindus and Moslems kill each other in India. In the Name of God, bloody warfare between Protestants and Catholics in Ireland. In the Name of God, Shiites and Sunnis are at each other's throats in Iraq and Iran, as are Arabs and Jews in the Middle East. In the name of God a doctor is murdered because he believed in a woman's right to choose. *In the Name of God, what is going on?*

As at no other time in recent memory, the issue of God has grown to such enormity that it can't be easily dismissed as the mental toy of theologians, fundamentalists, and all those others who take such talk seriously. Or as Stephen Carter has suggested: Has the time of "God as a hobby" finally come to an end?

I once shared with a new-members class that I define religion as the way we order or organize our lives in relationship to ultimate or holy meaning. That meaning, for many, is what God is. Suffice it to say that Alan Watts was probably right when he said that "that ultimate something which can't be defined or fixed can be represented by the word 'God.'" (*The Wisdom of Insecurity*) It's simply a representation, a word, a symbol—and it's not necessarily the word itself, but what's behind the word that counts. So, how we think about God becomes critical.

In his book, *Being Liberal in an Illiberal Age,* Jack Mendelsohn says that there are at least three ways that we think about God. These are really approaches, perspectives, boundary lines that are drawn. As with many other things, they are not exclusive, but interdependent circles.

First is "God and the search for meaning and purpose." In my experience, this is where most people begin, in one way or another. The need for meaning and purpose in life is fundamentally the religious quest, it's what religion is all about, whether you are religiously orthodox or liberal, whether you see yourself as a religious person or not.

For many of us (at least this is the path I followed), the first place we turned to was what we could know best—other people. For the longest time, I regarded myself as a religious humanist. And that word *religious* is critical because while I felt that humans are very important, I didn't go the point of saying that humans are the measure of all things. Yet then and now, I recognize that it's often difficult for me to see beyond the tip of my nose, which is to say that there are certain limitations to being merely human, one of which is a large dose of egocentricism or humanocentricism.

I am suggesting that the human community occupies a special place in this universe (which shouldn't be confused with special status). It only makes sense that we turn to each other, to our congregation for support, meaning, and purpose. And what's more, with Love (or God) as our bond, we have a commitment to one another that is unbreakable, unshakable, and undeniable. Anyone or any religion that makes light of this—or worse, any religion or person who seeks to break up the love of human community—risks undermining the very thing that holds us together. God and the search for meaning and purpose has strong roots in religious humanism. I'm sure that for many of us, the fellowship and love found in the community of people will always be a source of wellspring and hope, a source of religious inspiration and commitment.

Next Mendelsohn describes "God as an idealized reality." This approach to thinking about God is a little like the concert violinist who commented: "I have splendid music, a splendid violin, and a splendid bow. All I need to do is bring them together and get out of the way." Knowing God is there for the wanting—simply let it happen. Faith is always emerging, struggling to come into existence; don't block the process.

This requires an open mind, a desire and willingness to find new insights or truths in ways currently unknown. Read this story:

All the philosophers, divines, and doctors of the law were assembled in court for the trial of Mullah Nassruddin. The accusation was a serious one; he had been going from town to town, saying, "Your so-called religious leaders are ignorant and confused." So he was charged with heresy, the penalty for which was death.

"You may speak first," said the caliph.

The mullah was perfectly self-possessed. "Have paper and pen brought in," he said, "and give them to the ten wisest men in this august assembly."

To Nassruddin's amusement, a great squabble broke out among the holy men as to who was the wisest among them. When the contention died down and each of the chosen ten was equipped with paper and pen, the mullah said, "Have each of them write down the answer to the following question: What is matter made of?"

The answers were written down and handed to the caliph, who read them out. One said, "It is made of nothing." Another said, "Molecules." Yet another, "Energy." Others, "Light," "I do not know," "Metaphysical being," and so on.

Said Nassruddin to the caliph, "When they come to an agreement of what matter is, they will be fit to judge questions of the spirit. Is it not strange that they cannot agree on something that they themselves are made of, yet they are unanimous in their verdict that I am a heretic?"

Faith and belief are ever emerging; to get locked into one set of beliefs, or dogma, is crippling. So certain yet confused were the accusers of the mullah that they were a farce, a joke. In this sense, whether our belief is in religious conservatism or religious liberalism, each can become fundamentalism and with that, faith is choked to death. For a faith that is not growing, emerging, waiting to be realized, is a faith that is motionless, a faith reflected by a God which is stagnant. But a faith reflective of a God which is both freedom and trust is a faith willing to embrace the soon-to-be-discovered. Creeds, dogmas, indeed religions can weigh you down, tie you to a God and a faith that are both stifling and undesirable. When thinking about God as an idealized reality, were are involved in an emerging process wherein the goal is known but the outcome is undetermined, where the desire is strong but the course is somewhat unmapped.

Finally, Mendelsohn speaks of "God and psychology." Thinking about God in this way is an inner process. It is the understanding and feeling that we have for ourselves, as persons of worth, what some might call self-esteem. Yet it's more than this. Whether we see ourselves as children of God (however you think about God), or as integral pieces of the Cosmos, or as loving members of the human community, all of these suggest a measure of sacredness to every person. To violate this sacredness is a sacrilegious act. Quite often (and I would be interested in knowing the exceptions), people who have little or no self-worth are people who have had their personhood violated through abuse, oppression, repression—it goes on and on and the degrees vary, but the point is that the violated are not whole. Some would go so far as to say that no one is whole, that all of us are on journeys of self-exploration seeking wholeness, a unity of mind, body, and soul whose final result is knowing God. The quest for a congruent life, a balancing and recognition of the inner and the outer life, the sacred and the secular, into a wholeness that allows one to stay at peace—this is knowing God, and thinking about God and psychology can perhaps lead you there.

Let me jump back to where I started, with the problem of God. What I've discovered is that the problem isn't so much God as it is me and others like me who are often trying so hard to do things the right way that we practically stumble over ourselves. Not that there's a wrong way, which is why I like Nancy Mairs's perspective: "It never occurred to me that one might go to church not because one believed in God but precisely because one didn't, that in 'going through the motions' one might not be performing empty gestures but preparing a space into which belief could flood if it were going to." (*Ordinary Time*)

Okay, it's not as though I've put my waders on, anticipating the rising waters of faith to overtake me. What I do glean from her idea is the need to remain ready, a posturing of pregnant anticipation. In fact, I think this is the frame of mind and spirit with which one must come to church (if not all of life). Of course the fault could be mine, but when I hear people say that they couldn't find anything religious in the church service, I want to respond by saying, "It's too bad you didn't come prepared." This isn't to suggest that I'm never "off," or the choir is off, or something else. What it suggests is that it's a dialogue; church is not a passive or merely a reactive experience. You've got to be open, ready to embrace, ready to ask, "How high?" when you hear "Jump!"

Just how willing are you to thinking about God, to experiencing God? When the problem is God, there's a lot at stake. How you think about it could change the way you live your life.

God II

God is a word that we've come up with to describe what no other single word can. Just in that alone, the word is insufficient. The ancient Hebrews recognized this right off, and so they made their word for God unutterable: it was sacrilegious to say that word. So then they came up with a word that meant the word no one could say!

It's because of this kind of thinking that I've called myself everything from atheist to agnostic to pagan—all done, in part, as a reaction to the misuse, overuse, and perversion of the word *God*. The most profound abuse has been accomplished by orthodox Western religions that have accorded their God with humanlike qualities as well as raising God above nature. My God is neither anthropomorphic nor supernatural: to me it is absurd, meaningless, destructive, and oppresssive to conceputalize a higher power as having attributes like humanity has in addition to being above and outside what we know, see, and feel.

I often use the word *God* merely because it's from the common pool of representations, what is called language—but I don't like it because of all the connotations, the "baggage," that comes with it. My higher power or God is not of or in this world, it *is* the world. As such, it works for me; it makes sense to me socially, politically, and spiritually when I confess to a God that is the world, for God and the Cosmos are one—they are synonymous. God is everything I know and probably don't know; it is the process that keeps life as I know it working; it is the process that keeps my life working. The purpose of the Cosmos—of God—is simply to continue *itself,* not to designate one piece better or worse, not to reward and so support and nurture certain elements more than others. Its purpose is just to continue—with whatever it takes, however it might be done—to maintain the flow of balance in order to sustain life, its life, the ongoingness of the Cosmos. There are no favorites in this scheme, there are no privileged. The "preferred" are those who play their part to preserve life, to maintain the balance that makes it all work, that keeps everything living.

What throws this cosmological design off is the one piece in the grand scheme that has become aware of itself, aware of the whole shebang: human beings. It seems, in our historical, collective, finite wisdom, we chose to create an anthropomorphic, supernatural God (and a system of religion based on this) which has for centuries supported (in varying degrees) the destruction of the Cosmos, the destruction of the very thing which sustains life, which is life.

Now, I am well aware that for some there is an unfriendliness to my God, an impersonal, cold distance that does not make it receptive to human touch, contact, and feeling. I think that this is why the Western God was created—people needed something they felt more in common with, something they could understand, something from which they felt they could win sympathy and empathy. Yet for me, this is exactly what I feel I get from God the Cosmos: security, intimacy, understanding, all those humanlike qualities and projections that orthodoxy has bestowed on its creation.

When we are in touch with our spiritual life, we can feel the Cosmos, we can sense the flow of life in and around us, and we know when life is out of balance. A life of the spirit opens one to all of this. In embracing the spirit, we are moved into the flow of the Cosmos, the Life process, to God.

God III

"Some things will never change, some things will always be the same." (found in *Singing the Living Tradition*) I've been familiar with these words from Thomas Wolfe for a long time. It's the kind of reading that easily pops to mind when I'm struck with the timelessness of a moon-filled early morning, the freshness of a cool breeze on a scorching day, the cooing of a baby in a predominantly adult audience, the pounding crash of waves on a midnight shoreline, the ring of laughter amidst the silence of a late evening. Some of these things will never change—they were the same for my parents and theirs, for my children and, if they wish, for theirs. Back and forth through the generations, these things will always be the same.

There is a quality about living, Wolfe seems to be saying, a quality that goes beyond the superficial and ephemeral. It is eternal, it is forever, it will never die. And Wolfe is just one of thousands, perhaps millions, who attempts to put into words what I'm calling an enduring center. What generation, near or distant, primitive, emerging, or advanced, has not asked questions, given answers, and kept up the ongoing human tradition of searching for and naming an enduring center?

In this center there is no doubt, there is only unconditional trust. When all else is gone, when all else has passed, when all else has been lost or is no longer important, there is this center. This center is enduring, eternal in the sense that it simply is—there are no strings attached. This enduring center is the well that can refresh, it is the balm "that heals the sin-sick soul," it is what doesn't fail when all else has.

Years ago, I read an article about a group of college students who were demanding their rights to be poets. They claimed it was an entitlement, as students, as human beings, to be poets. The article was not defending, but castigating them. How ridiculous, the magazine writers insinuated, for there is no entitlement to being a poet—it comes with study, hard work, trial and error, more failure than success, and lots of criticism.

In this same vein, I wonder if any of us would claim an entitlement, a right to an enduring center. Is it something we all have access to, but is often denied because we haven't paid the dues? Is it too much to ask for what some have claimed is at the very core of our being, but easily can go unrecognized? Is it really fair that some are renewed and invigorated, born again and graced, inspired daily and inspiring to others just because they have found a way to an enduring center?

The quest for an enduring center is at the heart of religion. And the religious urge, I believe, is at the heart of every person—we all are religious. How we choose to express this religious life, whether or not we choose to do anything with it and about it, whether we choose to waste it, abuse it, or ignore it are decisions we all must make. When, how, and why we make the choices we do are determined by age, context, experience, and need. There can be many reasons that we come out in one place and somebody else in another. It won't always appear to make a lot of sense. But about this I am clear: that while the choice to honor our religious urging will take on unique, individual expression (which might include no expression at all), the presence of the religious spirit is as integral to our being as is the color of our eyes or the prints on our fingers.

For some this center has been found in the laws of science, for others in the love of a companion; for some this center has been realized in the interdependent web of the natural world, for others in the visual and performing arts; for some this center has been found in the God of their mothers and fathers, and for some in a God as unique and different to every person as is every grain of sand on every beach in the world; for some this center is unknown, unnamed, and untouched, and for others it is as personal and present as the air that sustains living; for some this center is a cruel hoax, mumbo-jumbo semantics, meaningless information, and for others it is a gift, it is the life that makes all things new.

The search for an enduring center can last a lifetime. It is and always has been a religious search—regardless of the name it goes by. May your search be one of depth and meaning.

Grace

While the word *grace* comes from the Christian tradition, the experience it names is common to virtually all religious and spiritual traditions. Charlene Spretnak says:

> When we experience consciousness or the unity in which we are embedded, the sacred whole that is and around us, we exist in a state of grace. At such moments our consciousness perceives not only our individual self, but also our larger self, the self of the cosmos. . . . Grace is considered by nearly all theologians to be a gift that is given. (*States of Grace*)

Unitarian Universalist minister Peter Fleck wrote:

> Grace is a blessing, a blessing that is undeserved, unsolicited, and unexpected, a blessing that brings a sense of the divine order into our lives. The ways of grace are mysterious, we cannot figure them out. But we know grace by its fruits, by the blessings of its works. (*Come As You Are*)

And finally, Frederick Beuchner adds this:

> If I were called upon to state in a few words the essence of everything I was trying to say both as a novelist and as a preacher, it would be something like this: Listen to your life. See it for the fathomless mystery that it is. In the boredom and pain of it no less than in the excitement and gladness: touch, taste, smell your way to the holy and hidden

heart of it because in the last analysis all moments are key moments, and life itself is grace. (*Listening to Your Life*)

In our culture, behind these three understandings of grace—a consciousness of unity, a sense of divine order, a listening to life—there stand thousands of years of history, reflecting several contexts for the blessings of grace to happen. Largely influenced by St. Augustine, Western Christianity sees grace as a private matter, almost entirely to do with individual sin and redemption. This is the theology from which the hymn "Amazing Grace" was written. Its author, John Newton, was an English slave trader. After being blessed with grace, he wrote: "Amazing grace! How sweet the sound that saved a wretch like me! I once was lost but now am found, was blind but now I see." And upon seeing, Newton left the sin of trafficking in human beings and shared his redemption by being an ardent supporter of abolition.

Eastern Orthodox Christianity believed grace was present throughout nature. The essence of this belief is captured so beautifully by Alice Walker in *The Color Purple* when Shug says:

> My first step from the old white man was trees. Then air. Then birds. Then other people. But one day when I was sitting quiet and feeling like a motherless child, which I was, it come to me: that feeling of being part of everything, not separate at all. I knew that if I cut a tree, my arm would bleed. And I laughed and cried and I run all around the house. I knew just what it was. In fact, when it happen, you can't miss it.

In our Unitarian Universalist heritage, we see the blending of Eastern Orthodoxy's grace in nature and Western Christianity's grace as a private matter in our transcendentalist roots, now emerging as contemporary paganism. The individual in nature is a major theme not just in Thoreau, Margaret Fuller, and Emerson, but in current writers. In fact, when I first read Richard Bode's essay from *First You Have to Row a Little Boat,* some lines of his sounded like they were straight from the shores of Walden Pond: "I once met a man," Bode writes, sounding just like Thoreau, "who said he had visited every exotic place from the Grand Canyon to the Great Wall, but when I questioned him closely I discovered he hadn't seen the songbirds of his own backyard." Bode, like the transcendentalists and today's pagans, is telling us that the blessings of grace are all around us. We just have to open our eyes and hearts.

This forms the core of a modern understanding of grace: it is unexpected—you don't know when the blessings will occur; it is undeserved—there's nothing you can do to earn grace; and yet it is everywhere, all about you—you don't have to be in the right place, timing means nothing.

But, Frederick Beuchner tells us, "There's only one catch. Like any other gift, the gift of grace can be yours only if you'll reach out and take it." As if driving in the fast lane of the expressway, Beuchner is suggesting that you've got to pull over, you've got to take your foot off the gas—which is all to say, you've got to do something.

Grace happens, if you'll reach out and take it. Hence the mystery that makes grace amazing: while on the one hand you can't do anything to force grace because grace happens, at the same time if you don't create the opportunity, if you're not open to it, if you're not willing to receive it, then there won't be grace.

Now, whether you want to think of grace in the Eastern, Western, transcendentalist, or modern context, I have some suggestions about taking the first step forward, ways to open the window so the warm winds of grace have the opportunity to blow in.

Call it centering, mindfulness, focusing—or maybe you've got another way to describe it—I believe we need to shut out all the background noise, the ongoing daily Muzak, the weekly distractions of life in the fast lane in an Information Age. To give grace a chance some meditate, others read or walk. I often get there when I jog; when I was a child it was early morning fishing on a lake. It's that time—almost like a sacred time—when for ten minutes or an hour, we ignore and disregard whatever fills our day. "If we fail," writes Bode, "we will pay for it with our lives. I mean that literally," he says, "for the consequences of indifference to the little wonders of the world are all too plain."

While we all will find our own way, I don't want us to dismiss the opportunities created for us in community. Too often we think of religious experience as a private, individualistic thing. So we undervalue or dismiss outright corporate contexts, like church, as opportunities for grace to be experienced. But for me—and maybe this is why I do what I do—I feel as though I have had some of the most powerful, grace-filled moments while in my congregation. There are times during community activities— like marches to the state house, hikes through the woods, even after a big church-sponsored event—when momentary glimpses of grace consciousness have poked through. Charlene Spretnak describes another important event for me and many others:

> Sometimes the consciousness of grace comes on quite suddenly and so intensely that the moment is never forgotten. More frequently, we experience slight versions of it, as in the act of group singing when the alignment of vibrations evokes in us awareness of the vibratory ocean of flux and form in and around us. Touching the ultimate truth in that way, and many others, brings us joy, release, connection, and peace.

Whether it's in a private or a corporate setting, I can't separate the blessings of grace from knowing and experiencing unconditional affirmation. Part of that blessing— a sense of divine order, a consciousness of unity, a listening to life—is knowing, believing, and telling that, in Jesse Jackson's words, "I am somebody." But it almost seems like we've gone in just the opposite direction: I hear stories from the classroom to office, from the dinner table to dates, from legislatures to board rooms of back-stabbing, disrespect, running people down. All of this runs contrary to the blessing of grace.

As with Unitarian Universalism, grace is the affirmation that worth and dignity are inherent to who we are as human beings. Regardless of the mistakes we make, the tensions we might create, regardless of what society might tell us, we know we are valued. In more orthodox language, this is what a Christian means when they share what was once the distinguishing message of Universalism, a message characterized by Frederick Beuchner like this:

> The grace of God means something like: Here is your life. You might never have been, but you are because the party wouldn't have been complete without you. Here is the world. Beautiful and terrible things will happen. Don't be afraid. I am with you. Nothing can ever separate us. It's for you I created the universe. I love you.

That's a very powerful message—perhaps overwhelming—in part because of the negative messages we can't seem to turn off; the larger culture's gospel that preaches that our worth, our value, is measured by what we think, what we produce, the color of our skin, our age, our gender, our sexual orientation. Society reminds us that we are not affirmed merely for being human. But the blessings of grace declare and affirm the inherent worth and dignity of every person.

I am convinced that children, especially young children, experience the blessing of grace—an affirming, unifying, and ordered consciousness—far more than adults do. The divisions of life and the logical reductionisms of the natural world that we as adults take pride in (and hope that our children will learn) are often foreign to them. For children the barriers to grace are not as many. What we spend time relearning—how to embrace the natural world and people—they take for granted. It's just that they don't talk about it because what they experience doesn't feel out of the ordinary. For them, grace isn't amazing, in fact it might be rather routine. It's only after they've been taught by adults that they slowly relinquish their grace-filled experiences, only wanting to recapture them again when they reach middle age.

How many times do we have the opportunity of grace and we miss it, we don't see or feel it, we dismiss it as just the everyday, the commonplace, the usual, no big deal. Mary Oliver is one of those transcendentalist poets who reminds us to take notice of the small things. Here's her poem called "The Sun":

> Have you ever seen / anything / in your life / more wonderful / than the way the sun / every evening, / relaxed and easy, / floats toward the horizon / and into the clouds or the hills, / or the rumpled sea, / and is gone— / and how it slides again / out of the blackness, / every morning, / on the other side of the world, / like a red flower / streaming upward on its heavenly oils, / say, on a morning in early summer, / at its perfect imperial distance— / and have you ever felt for anything / such wild love— / do you think there is anywhere, in any language, / a word billowing enough / for the pleasure / that fills you, / as the sun / reaches out, / as it warms you / as you stand there, / empty-handed— / or have you too / turned from this world— / or have you too / gone crazy / for power, / for things?

The blessings of grace—a consciousness of unity, a sense of divine order, a listening to life—will come only when you're not focused on the big experience. It comes when it isn't forced, it comes in the everyday.

Mary Oliver asks: "Do you think there is anywhere, in any language, a word billowing enough for the pleasure that fills you as the sun reaches out. . . ." Yes, there is such a word. Grace happens. Know it, believe it, tell it. Grace happens.

High Holy Days

Atonement, sin, forgiveness, confession, repentance—this is the language of the High Holy Days, of Yom Kippur. There is no page in the Unitarian Universalist handbook that explains these in a language translated for us. Besides, to take forgiveness and repentance as serious religious categories and practices assumes that you've got something to be forgiving/forgiven about, that our religious community might have something credible to contribute to your living, forgiving, and repenting. How I make sense of all of this follows.

Every field of interest or concern has its own vocabulary, be it medicine, engineering, education, law, sports, music, or others. So does religion. The words used during the High Holy Days come from the religious dictionary. It's just that as religious liberals, as Unitarian Universalists, we have chosen not to recognize or use all the words in that dictionary—even though we share it. The difficulty is that this dictionary, as with all dictionaries, has been updated—added to, taken away from, and reinterpreted. The religious dictionary has been updated by religious Orthodoxy and fundamentalism, which have defined and redefined the words in ways that no longer hold meaning for us.

Sin is a good example. Christian Orthodoxy and fundamentalism have co-opted this word and used it in a way that suggests flawed personhood; whatever it is that is most basic about being a person is messed up, and in some cases is evil. But the older, Jewish understanding of sin means "to miss the mark," which suggests that to sin is to not live up to what we know we can do, our potential.

And then, of course, there's God. Just the notion that you can define God in a way that is acceptable to all is absolutely ridiculous—perhaps sacrilegious. But certainly this is what the Christian Orthodoxy and fundamentalists have done—and if you don't accept their definition of God and use it in their approved way, well then, obviously you aren't religious! Among Unitarian Universalists, there are probably as many definitions or understandings about God as there are members and friends. So while we couldn't affirm the same definition of God, I do believe that we could (and do) admit a personal and communal responsibility and accountability to Something larger than ourselves. That Something will go by names that sound scientific, ecological, philosophical, even traditional—but in each case, this God is larger than life or is Life. I like the way Vaclav Havel, the poet and playwright who became the president of the Czech Republic, framed it. He calls this God the Community of Memory, in front of whom we must all live and die and make an accounting of our living.

Then there's forgiveness and confession. As I've gotten older the impact and value of these two have grown in importance. When I was younger I simply didn't see anything very wrong that I'd done; it was all repairable, it was no big deal. But now I know differently: there are people who have been hurt, decisions that were wrong, mistakes made that hurt not just others, but me. And what do I do with all of that? More and more, the importance of a confessing community has been vital for me, the idea that there is sometime in my week when I have an opportunity to assess and reflect on the knowledge that there is another way, that I will fall short, and others do too. These have all become important to my coming and going. Friend and colleague Don Wheat put these thoughts like this:

> Perhaps at one time we thought of forgiveness as some great virtue, some luxury that we could bestow upon others.

But the longer we live, the more we see it as a simple necessity, something that we do *for ourselves* more than we do for others. (*In Pursuit of Joy*)

When it comes to forgiveness and confession, I still find value and meaning in those words and in their practice; I find them powerful and healing in the religious community; and I resent having to use a page out of someone else's dictionary as a guide to being religious.

While the five steps to be observed during the High Holy Days focus on forgiveness, confession, and repentance, there is more. The theme of these ten days is really compassion and transformation—the five steps are merely a way to get there. Forgiveness and confession are just opportunities to examine what you've been doing with life, a way to acknowledge what you've done and then to get on with it. You dwell on it for ten days, you make note of it, then you start over. Compassion, transformation, and liberation—these are the results of the High Holy Days and they are embraced in this story:

Two monks on a pilgrimage came to the ford of a river. There they saw a girl dressed in all her finery, obviously not knowing what to do since the river was high and she did not want to spoil her clothes. Without more ado, one of the monks took her on his back, carried her across and put her down on dry ground on the other side.

Then the monks continued on their way. But after an hour the other monk started complaining, "Surely it is not right to touch a woman; it is against the commandments to have close contact with women. How could you go against the rules of monks?"

The monk who had carried the girl walked along silently, but finally he remarked, "I set her down by the river an hour ago. Why are you still carrying her?"

After a certain point, you can't continue dwelling on what might have been wrong, which is so often the message heard from Orthodoxy and fundamentalism. Yet of course moving on, liberation, will be shallow and cheap unless there is a sincere effort made to set things right. And so, with forgiveness and confession, by observing the five steps of the High Holy Days—remember, resolve, reconcile, confess, and resist—compassion and transformation can happen, we can move from the way things are to the way things ought to be. Compassion and transformation—this is what living life with religious integrity is all about. *Tikkun olam* is the Hebrew for the transformation and healing of the world. "All the rest," said Rabbi Hillel, "is commentary."

Forgiveness and confession, compassion and transformation—in a way, we're talking about salvation, another of those words from the religious dictionary, another of those words that we religious liberals jettisoned when the Orthodoxy and fundamentalists told us what it meant. Salvation is about saving ourselves, saving our communities, saving our world—it's about transforming life from what is into what ought to be.

In this spirit, here are some reflections based on words written by Christian theologian Reinhold Niebuhr, who put the whole business of saving ourselves in a very Jewish way:

"Nothing worth doing is completed in our lifetime; therefore, we are saved by hope," our hope for a future that witnesses what we worked and stood for, that the way things are is not the way things have to be.

"Nothing true or beautiful or good makes complete sense in any immediate context of history; therefore we are saved by faith," a faith in the enduring worth and dignity and integrity of what we value as true and meaningful.

"Nothing we do, however virtuous, can be accomplished alone; therefore. we are saved by love," the love of people willing and working and believing together.

"No virtuous act is quite as virtuous from the standpoint of our friend or foe as from our own; therefore, we are saved by the final form of love which is forgiveness," forgiveness for missing the mark, a forgiveness that frees us to transform and begin again in love.

Hope

The Latin word for hope is *sperare,* which comes from an Indo-European root meaning 'to expand'. To be of hope means to feel expansive, to feel no constraint; to go beyond the limits and embrace a wider view, to think beyond the boundaries. For me, hope epitomizes the Unitarian Universalism I have come to know and love. And if I had to use just one word as synonymous with my understanding of who and what we are as a faith community—not just today but for our history—it would be hope. I see and feel hope in these ways.

The hope that is Unitarian Universalism lives in the present with an eye to the future. I thought about this when I recently read this story:

> A British couple in their mid-twenties, haggard and bruised, recalled for the television camera how they were on holiday in Indonesia, trying to decide whether to get married, when the ferryboat they were riding between islands sank during a storm. They clambered into a lifeboat, but so did many others, and the lifeboat foundered. So the couple set off swimming, calling back and forth to keep track of one another in the rough seas, until they came upon a floating spar, and there they clung, waiting for rescue. Eventually five other passengers joined them; but one by one the others ran out of strength, let go of the spar and drowned. Asked how they managed to hold on for thirteen hours while the waves hurled them about, the couple smiled shyly at the camera. The woman says, We remembered things we'd done together, we told jokes, we sang. We promised one another we'd get

married straightaway, the man says, if only we survived. It seemed almost like a test, the woman says, as though some great power had asked us a question. How could we let go? (told by Russell Sanders in *Hunting for Hope*)

The hope that I experience in Unitarian Universalism doesn't permit me to let go of what we share, the shared meaning that keeps me afloat. Grounded in the present, in the everyday, in the here-and-now experiences of daily living, I know what could be and I'm willing to work with others to transform the here and now based on a shared vision—a vision that we laugh and sing about, that we argue and cry about, a vision that if we are to reach it can only be arrived at together. The hope that is Unitarian Universalism asks, "How can you let go?"

The hope that is Unitarian Universalism is about possibility. As Unitarian Universalists, our faith speaks of anticipation and expectancy as though living on the edge of our seats. *Hope* and *hop* come from the same root that suggests leaping in expectation. Now, I know that we are not given to authentic Sunday morning emotive outbursts driven by whatever spirit moves us. I'm reminded of the northern urban Unitarian church that was visited by a rural southern Universalist. In the middle of the sermon, the southern Universalist, who was moved by the sermon's words of expectation and possibility, leaped from his pew and shouted, "Amen, sister, amen. You preach the liberal word!" At that point one of the ushers came running down the aisle to ask if the man was okay. "Okay? I'm doing just fine, mighty fine. I'm filled with hope, Mr. Usher. I can feel the hope of my faith"—to which the usher replied, "Well that's well and good, but not now, not here."

Unitarian Universalism has always asked in its message of hope, If not now, then when? If not here, where? Of course now and here! Our faith preaches a message of expectation, of possibility, of hope. Let us live this hope and move to the edge of our seats with anticipation, prepared to hop when moved by our spirit!

The hope that is Unitarian Universalism assumes the best about people. As a voluntary, covenantal faith community, we assume that people are here because they want to be, that you are here in the spirit of fellowship, that we have each others' best interests in mind. Sometimes this can be a mixed blessing because the hope that is Unitarian Universalism doesn't give up on people. Our hope puts faith in people's ability, goodness, and possibility—in their potential. Wherever a person is on their faith journey, we want to empower, not silence. In a different context, Maya Angelou tells this story:

> When I was seven, I was sent to St. Louis where my mother's [family took me in, and it was while there that her] boyfriend raped me. I was afraid to tell his name because the man said he would kill my brother. Well, my brother was then—and is now—my black kingdom come. I told him. The man was put in jail, released in one day, and in three days he was found dead. So I thought that my voice, my mouth, killed him. I stopped speaking for six years. My mother's family didn't know what to do with me . . . so they sent me back to Stamps, Arkansas, to Mama.
> Mama would say, "Your Mama don't care what these people say about you. Mama know, when you and the good Lord get ready, you're going to be a preacher. You're going to be somebody." I used to think, That poor, ignorant woman. But here I am. Everybody else had given me up. Not only was I black and female and poor, but raped, a mute in a little village in Arkansas. That was love, it was hope. (*Restoring Hope*)

I know that many come to Unitarian Universalism having been silenced by a version of religious or spiritual rape, and like Angelou, they need support and encouragement as they learn that it's safe to speak again—to speak of their meaning, their God, their vision and journey—in a community that will honor and love them for who they are and not what they should be. This is the hope called Unitarian Universalism.

So, I've been sharing with you all about this hope that is our faith. And by what authority, you might wonder— I mean, maybe you are wondering how I know. I will only begin an answer. I will start with these words from

Vaclav Havel as though they were mine: "I have thought about this and examined myself a thousand times, and eventually—to the delight of some and the astonishment of others—I have always come to the conclusion that the primary origin of hope is, to put it simply, metaphysical. By that I mean to say that hope is more, and goes deeper, than a mere optimism or disposition of the human mind." It is to say that hope comes from inside us. I don't believe we get hope somewhere along the way: we already have it, each one of us, and it's just a matter of figuring out how to feel it, use it, experience hope. For me, it's Unitarian Universalism that best does it because our faith makes this hope its starting place.

You see, we begin by acknowledging a version of this maybe silly, but simple story:

It's told that when God finished with Creation, She had a desire to leave something behind, just a small piece of divinity and wholeness so humans could experience this delight. But God was a bit of trickster too, so She didn't want this to be too easy for human beings. She wasn't sure, at first, where to put this special something, so she asked the other living things in creation. Someone suggested in the stars and God replied, No, I have this feeling that that might be too easy. Some day humans will explore space and they will find it. Someone else suggested hiding it in the depths of the ocean. God thought about it for a moment and answered, No, She also had a feeling that one day humankind would explore the deepest places in the seas—that was also too easy. Then suddenly, God had it. "I know where I'll put this special something, a place where they will never look. I'll hide it in them, they will never look there." And so it was. And so it has been.

While it goes by many different names, I have chosen to call it Hope. We each have it—without it, we cannot live. It is the essence of our faith. Let us trust it, for in doing that, our spirits can soar.

Humanism

After the 1961 merger of Unitarianism and Universalism, liberal religious humanism unknowingly found itself drifting into a position of liberal orthodoxy. "Unknowingly" because it would take at least several decades before the anti-orthodoxy grumblings would become loud enough to be heard. It would also take decades before many religious humanists—like myself—could look back and see what was happening: that a creeping humanist orthodoxy had taken over. Richard Erhardt shares his understanding and experience in an essay:

> Because of its largely unexamined set of assumptions, which is a luxury only a dominant group can afford, I use the term orthodoxy deliberately. Orthodoxy means right thinking. From our inception [in 1961] to the present any right thinking Unitarian Universalist leaned towards humanistic understandings of the world. When I was growing up I learned that it was all right to say just about anything that was on my mind in my UU congregation. But that right ended if I mentioned the word God. That right ended if I pondered an afterlife. That right ended if I ventured out of Newtonian physics toward the quantum models and its implications which strongly point away from a modernistic humanism toward a post-modern understanding of life. I had an experiential understanding of humanism as an orthodoxy. As a teenager and as a young adult, when I challenged the unexamined assumptions the reaction was similar to positing a round earth when anyone can plainly see that it's flat. *(First Day's Record)*

Erhardt's description parallels my experience with one congregation I worked closely with, a congregation of 150 members and 125 children and youth in the church school that was considering full-time professional ministry. It was the first time I experienced anticlericalism and rampant hostility for honest, open theological dialogue. "Trashing" the religious right—which was anyone who didn't accept the dogma of secular humanism—was popular sport that most seemed to enjoy and participate in with unquestioning allegiance. Though this congregation eventually softened its approach (to both clergy and theological conversation), it was the first of many experiences that would shake my support for Unitarian Universalist religious humanism. There would be other experiences similar to this one, as well as conversations with colleagues who were as entrenched and narrow in their views as that congregation. Finally, as others have said, I too found myself in the awkward and uncomfortable place of being an identified and outspoken religious humanist who was becoming increasingly dissatisfied, frustrated, and unhappy with a well-entrenched, parochial religious humanism that had become illiberal, that is, it had put parameters on religious experience and discussion, which was one of the reasons I had become a Unitarian Universalist. In short, I felt betrayed.

Why? What happened? At least two things. First, as we left the civil turmoil and strife of the 1960s and 1970s, and got beyond the navel-gazing of the 1980s, many (the baby boomers especially, but not exclusively) began looking for something other than the Cold War neo-Protestantism of the 1950s and 1960s or the existential relativism and political activism of the 1970s and 1980s. Religious humanism had an active place in all three of these. As the church, in general, lost its appeal and members during the 1960s through the 1970s, so did the Unitarian Universalist religious humanism that had sustained us for so many years. By the end of the 1980s and entering the 1990s, Unitarian Universalist religious humanism was simply losing its meaning for many. Similar to the Unitarian Christians of the mid-nineteenth century who were unwilling to accept and make room for the needs, beliefs, and ideals of the younger, free-thinking Unitarians, Unitarian Universalist religious humanists appeared to lock out those whose faith sounded as if it were outside the boundaries they had drawn as defining Unitarian Universalism. This then led to a second step that would mark orthodox religious humanism's downturn: again, like the orthodoxy that controlled an earlier religious liberal era, organized religious humanism did very little to compromise or embrace those who felt themselves outside the faith core. As some once appealed to the memory of William Ellery Channing, today's religious humanists conjure up the memories of history's strong religious humanists and appeal, in their names, for a religion grounded in the three Rs: reason, rationality, and responsibility.

I believe that most Unitarian Universalists would be surprised to learn that some feel the need to return to reason, rationality, and responsibility. My sense is that most Unitarian Universalists would agree that there is still plenty of this to go around several times, which is in part an indication of the fact that a majority of Unitarian Universalists still identify themselves as—or at least have strong sympathies for—religious humanists, as I still do. The core of our faith, at least in name, has not changed.

But the players, expression, and borders have changed. It's not religious humanism versus theism or humanism versus spirituality, as the traditional characterization of the debate suggests. It's competing versions of religious humanism. It appears that one group is the religious humanists that brought us to this point. The other I'll call the free religious humanists. They too start out with the three Rs, but don't want barriers and limitations—they don't want anyone telling them that they can only go so far and if they go beyond that, then the perspective or label of religious humanist doesn't fit, or as others have suggested, then one isn't even a Unitarian Universalist!

This is a new version of religious humanism. It is a religious humanism that continues to value the role of science and asserts that orthodox religious belief and practice must be reformed—transformed—by modern and current insights. These insights, though, include a broad range of ritual, practice, and belief; story, myth, and study.

What I embrace as the new religious humanism is a promise of the sort that first attracted me to Unitarian Universalism: the promise of very broad boundaries. I believe that this broadness is what accounts for the satisfaction and depth that has been the leading edge of our association's nearly decade-long growth at a time when other "mainline" groups have lost members. My experience is that most of my congregation's new members come for many of the same reasons I came: reason, rationality, responsibility, and an opportunity and a promise of religious and spiritual openness to explore and journey in the company of others. They too come as what I would call religious humanists.

Most of these newcomers know very little of the humanism that brought us to this point. They come with a desire to explore, a willingness to listen and learn, and the hope for religious depth, support, and exhilaration. In Victoria Safford's words, they come wanting to be "a human being, trying to discern and describe the beautiful, the good, the true, and to effect these, to the extent [they] can, in the world." *(World: The Journal of the Unitarian Universalist Association)* To me, this sounds like they come for the progressive liberalism of religious humanism cast in a new language.

The new religious humanism uses the language of balance, of balancing left and right sides of the brain, of deconstructing dualisms in order to honor the interdependent web, of breaking up (but not eliminating) the century-old mantra of reason, rationality, and responsibility with myth, soul, ritual, and spirit. This is a religious humanism for a new century, a new millennium. This will be the core of our Unitarian Universalist faith.

Idolatry

I am well aware that in many liberal religious circles, definitions and discussions of God are frowned on if not outright dismissed or silently banned. (Did you hear about the Unitarian Universalist mountain climber who slipped off a precipice and was falling to his death when he grabbed onto a protruding root? Panicked, he called up to the place from which he slipped and cried, "Is anybody up there to help me?" And a voice replied, "Yes. It is I. God." The Unitarian Universalist thought a second and shouted back, "Anybody else?") Confusion, division, and doubt often rule the roost. I agree with what Sam Keen suggests in *Hymn to an Unknown God:* "The question of God is not the question of the existence of some remote infinite being. It is the question of the possibility of hope. . . . To deny God is equivalent to denying any ground for hope." God and Hope are one and the same, they are synonymous. And so for me, to be without Hope is to be an atheist; or even more poignantly, to call oneself an atheist is to live without Hope, which means that whatever faith the atheist has is a faith in things—the practice of idolatry.

Years ago, a professor challenged me around this issue. It was during a theological discussion where I kept trying to frame our debate as theism versus atheism. He finally shared that he really didn't think this was it—it was theism versus idolatry, and it was then that he said: "We all worship something, we all have our gods—what are yours?" Not idolatry, but Hope. Ken Bode comments, in *First You Have to Row a Little Boat:*

> When we kill the [hope] within us, we kill ourselves, even though the blood continues to flow through our veins. We can see the signs of this living death about us everywhere: in shopping malls, in discount and department stores. . . . We see people scurrying compulsively, buying compulsively, as if they hoped through the expenditure of money, the acquisition of goods, to deaden a pain they don't even know they have.
>
> I know a couple who uses shopping to dispel an unyielding sadness that seems to overwhelm them day by day. Whenever their depression becomes more than they can bear, they buy new furniture for their living room. And it helps—for a while. But in due course the sadness engulfs them again, and they don't know why.

Whether it's shopping or any of the other countless things for us to put our energies and faith into, the distractions and detours are many. The ruts that we can fall into are worn deep and wide by history, bitterness, societal approval, as well as ignorance. If we didn't see dramatic and daring examples, we might think that the power and reality of Hope were impossible and that idolatry rules the day.

Jesus

As Unitarian Universalists, the Christian heritage is our heritage; Jesus is part of our religious history and tradition; we observe and celebrate the Christmas message and meaning. So where does Jesus fit in? What do we do with this central and critical person and his story? How do we read that story? With original intent? With current, personal understanding?

Over the last decade, there's been a lot of attention focused on the work of the Jesus Seminar, a group with an approach that has found a following among Unitarian Universalists and other religious liberals. You might say that they epitomize the school of original intent. Here's who they are and how they work:

The Jesus Seminar is composed of scholars and academics dedicated to uncovering the authentic words and actions of Jesus, rather than the interpreted or mythological. Bringing their particular expertise, knowledge, and background to each meeting, they use a ritualized procedure for arriving at consensus on the agenda items at that meeting. Debate and discussion are held on the topic of the day and then they vote. Using this approach over the last several years, the Jesus Seminar has determined that 410 (82 percent) of the approximately 500 words attributed to Jesus are not authentic. For example:

> The parable of the Good Samaritan was probably authentic to Jesus as are ten other stories. Another ten parables are probably inauthentic.

It is unlikely Jesus called the bread and wine his body and blood at the Last Supper.

Jesus probably did not ask why God had forsaken him or ask God to forgive his persecutors.

Jesus did not publicly proclaim himself the Messiah.

Jesus probably did not speak the Lord's Prayer or most of the Beatitudes.

He probably never claimed he would come again. (*World: The Journal of the Unitarian Universalist Association*)

This is just the kind of thing that many Unitarian Universalists love! It's interesting, intriguing, very rational, and gives plenty of ammunition for any religious liberal wishing to take on the next door-to-door or family evangelist.

But then, another reaction I had was, "So, what?" So what if Jesus did or didn't do or say some of these things. What difference does it really make? These are the types of responses that you'll hear given not by those pursuing the historical Jesus, but those who already have their minds made up. For them, it's a matter of faith, faith in Jesus—and what a group of scholars have to say, what archeologists may unearth in an Egyptian field, what they discover decades from now, makes no difference at all. It's a matter of faith: either you believe or you don't. All of this is summarized by Claudia Setzer, who wrote in *Tikkun:*

Both the church and academia have gotten along successfully without the historical Jesus for centuries. The historical Jesus, the human being who walked the roads of ancient Israel, gathered disciples, and was executed by the Romans, is often contrasted with the "Christ of faith," a supra-historical figure whose presence in the world enlivens and nourishes Christian communities. The latter has always been far more important for most Christians.

But we are not Christians, we are Unitarian Universalists, and while there are some who might identify with our Christian heritage more than others (just as there are those who identify more strongly with our Jewish heritage), we still are a people of faith, a Unitarian Universalist faith community whose roots are in both the Jewish and Christian traditions. We cannot simply dismiss the life of Jesus as unimportant or inconsequential, whether by using the decrees of the Jesus Seminar or other sources. At the same time, believing for the sake of believing—a blind faith in spite of original intent or historical context—this doesn't cut it either, and never has. What both groups hold in common is a respect, interest, and reverence for Scripture and the life story of Jesus. It's out of these that I think that there is a balance to be found. Using a little of the historical approach tempered with strong belief we can find a middle ground, a balanced understanding, meaning, and faith.

For example, there's been a lot said and written about trying to distinguish the religion of and taught by Jesus from the religion about Jesus. The religion of Jesus is one that cannot be separated from who he was and the culture in which he lived, which can be summed up in one word: Jewish. To try to do anything other than this is simply wrong. Jesus was a Jew and it was out of his Jewish background that he taught and listened; his audience was Jewish and what they heard and listened for is something quite different from what Christians today choose to hear. Jesus was killed as a Jew for disrupting the civic and religious order of his day. On the other hand, the religion that has grown up around Jesus is something quite different: the trinity, the Nicene and Athanasian creeds, the Westminster Confession, and hundreds of other creeds, dogmas, rituals, and symbols have all been added by councils, leaders, and tribunals. This is all the religion about Jesus, something he knew nothing of.

In 1841, it was our own Theodore Parker who preached a sermon entitled, "The Transient and the Permanent in Christianity," which was on this very issue: separating the religion about Jesus (the transient) from the religion of Jesus (the permanent). And years before that, Unitarian Thomas Jefferson produced his "Jefferson Bible," which consists of only Jesus' teachings, not the miracles and other commentary. In the early part of this century, Unitarian and suffragette Elizabeth Cady Stanton edited a woman's Bible.

For Parker, Jefferson, Stanton, and so many others before and since, even their awareness of the religion about Jesus didn't diminish their respect for or faith in what he symbolized, taught, and meant. If anything, taking the historical, original-intent approach bolstered their radical belief and strengthened their faith, something that could be as true for us as it was for them.

Another example of a balanced approach: the historical search tells us that Jesus was part of a popular messianic tradition of that time. It was an era when Jews believed that the coming of the anointed one, the Messiah, could be any day. The Messiah's arrival would mark the coming of the Kingdom of God and the end of life on earth as they knew it. As a Jew, there can be no doubt that this is the context that Jesus spoke to, this was the expectation of those who followed him. Try to imagine how some might have responded to the messianic messages of those days. I mean, Jesus was just one of many declaring the Kingdom of God to be at hand. There's a modern-day rendition of a couple who were challenged by this message: A wealthy farmer burst into his home one day and cried out in an anguished voice, "Rebecca, there is a terrible story in town—the Messiah is here!

"What's so terrible in that?" asked the wife. "I think it's great. What are you so upset about?"

"What am I so upset about?" the man exclaimed. "After all these years of sweat and toil, we have finally found prosperity. We have a thousand head of cattle, our barns are full of grain, and our trees laden with fruit. Now we will have to give it all away and follow him."

"Calm down," said his wife consolingly. "The Lord our God is good. God knows how much we Jews have always had to suffer. We had a Pharaoh, a Haman, a Hitler—always somebody. But our dear God found a way to deal with them all, right? Just have faith, my dear husband, God will find a way to deal with the Messiah too."

The discomfort of the messianic proclamation in Jewish culture—whether 2,000 years ago or today, as this

story suggests—was very different from what it was to become in Christian culture. The Kingdom of God was not a
heavenly, out-of-this-world, by-salvation-only, end of life.
It was a new order on this earth, it was liberation from
oppression where the first would be last and the last
first; God would afflict the comfortable and comfort the
afflicted—which is to say, it would be a real change in
everyday lifestyle! It was a message for this world, about
life in this world. It was not the promise of eternal life or
life in the hereafter, it was about living in the here and
now. That was the threat. That's why Jesus had to be put
to death. If he'd been preaching about a life somewhere
other than in this world, that would have been no problem. But that's not what he was talking about. His message, his life, was about becoming and nurturing the
Beloved Community among us, now. It was about the inherent worth and dignity of every person, a message
about justice, equality, and compassion in human relations; he preached and practiced acceptance of one another. These were the qualities of the Kingdom of God, the
Beloved Community—and Jesus' gospel was one that neither religious nor political leaders wanted to hear.

Balancing the religion about Jesus with the religion of
Jesus, balancing the context in which Jesus preached his
messianic gospel of the Beloved Community with the
faith that this community will become a reality, these are
important not only for the modern Christian, but for today's Unitarian Universalists. We too need to balance
what we believe is historically accurate with what our age
and faith demand, declaring neither one as the way or
that one cancels out the other. There is a lot of accuracy
and insight in what Albert Schweitzer wrote in his semi-
nal work *The Quest of the Historical Jesus,* a classic that
is still required reading for many seminarians. He says:
"Jesus as a concrete historical personality remains a
stranger to our time, but His spirit, which lies hidden in
his words, is known in simplicity, and its influence is
direct. Every saying contains in its own way the whole
Jesus." The way Claudia Setzer puts it: "Each group and

generation sees in Jesus a reflection of itself," because, as Schweitzer says, the whole Jesus is in every saying.

This how and why Unitarian Universalists can find meaning, relevance, support, and direction in the gospel according to Jesus, his life and words. His message is as powerful today as it was then, if we are willing to read the Gospels with balance, if we are willing to read with a sense of history guided by faith.

Joy (Genesis 28:10–17)

The human spirit, the Dionysian urge, is not rational, but irrational—something I grew up believing was negative. When some have heard me remark that I wonder if people think too much, that we try to be too rational, I get these stares as if to ask: "How can you be too rational?" We generally think of someone who's irrational as a person who's unusual, strange, insane—definitely not somebody with whom we want to spend much time. But irrational originally meant knowledge received through our senses rather than through logical thought processes. This is a pretty fitting description of what I'm calling the human spirit: it's sensual, irrational; logic isn't its standard. The point is to feel good, to be ecstatic, to experience joy. The human spirit's home is not in the head, but the soul, in the depths of our being-ness.

I, maybe like you, spend most of my days in my head, with the rational, the logical. That's the way I've been taught. I was not raised as a feeling person, sensual, aware of and in touch with my irrational side, with my spirit. I've had to discover this, lose my fear of it, embrace it, and nurture it all on my own. And it hasn't come easy. I've been brainwashed into believing that the point of life is to be happy. I found myself in a place similar to that of Robert Johnson, who realized he wasn't sure what all these words meant—they seemed nearly interchangeable. To his surprise, he "found that 'happiness' was defined as 'a happening of chance, luck, fortune'. . . . Happiness was always short-lived. We think we should be happy—after all, isn't the pursuit of happiness guaranteed to us in the Bill of Rights? But happiness comes at the whim of fortune. No happiness can be kept permanently." (*Ecstasy*)

On the other hand, he found that joy was an "exultation of the spirit, gladness, delight, the beatitude of heaven or paradise. Joy is what the human spirit expresses. Happiness is found "out there," in the passing of things. You latch onto it and take it in—use it while it serves a purpose, and then in all probability, discard it after a point. But joy comes from inside, from the depths of feeling, from your spirit, out of your soul. Joy is sitting in there just waiting—bubbling like a sleeping yet active volcano, just waiting for the right conditions, whether it's appropriate or not. In other words, it's there, the irrational side of us all is there, that sensual, feeling, exuberant joy is there—it's called ecstasy. Maybe you've felt it, experienced it—perhaps it was fleeting and you'd like to feel that way again. Mere happiness won't do it.

Jacob got the wake-up call, as told in Genesis 28. There he was in a godforsaken place, the last place he ever expected to have anything good happen. And he has this most incredible dream. He wakes up shaken by it, maybe even a bit frightened, and he realizes that where he is is sacred—and he didn't even know it, he wasn't aware of it. So he says: "Surely the Lord is in this place; and I did not know it. How awesome is this place! This is none other than the house of God, and this is the gate of heaven."

The biblical author is telling us something about pure joy: if you're not aware of it, you'll let the chance go right by. I wonder how many times I've missed the obvious. A good friend of mine constantly is telling me how complicated I make life: "It's really not that hard, Fred." His sentiment rings in my ears. Living is meant to be joyful—we carry it around with us, it's here for the wanting. Why do we keep missing it, messing with it? Jacob's story tells us: Wake up! Become fully present, pay attention to what's going on, for the place where you stand (or sit, or lie) is holy ground—the gate of heaven. I heard someone remark that many people go through life constantly hitting the snooze alarm, which means they're never really fully awake. Perhaps this is what Kierkegaard means when he says that our age will die not from sin, but from a lack of passion.

What an absolutely horrible thought. I could think of no greater condemnation, no greater curse than to be accused of being passionless. To me this means to lack feeling, compassion, emotion, to have no joy. To be passionless is to say you have no spirit, your soul is dead. I would rather die sinning passionately. Passion and the passion of joy are basic to our humanness. If nothing else, I want to live and to die fully human.

It's so hard to express, though—I get stymied, I come up short. And what to me seems like the irony of all ironies is that if ever there was a single place where the human spirit of passion and joy should and could be expressed, it's the church, because the spirit, basic human beingness, is what we are all about. If joy—the irrational—isn't welcomed in church, then where? But look at so many congregations: it's another head-trip, just like the rest of the week.

Now, there's good reason for this. Historically, as a backlash against the Greek god of joy and ecstasy, Dionysius, the early Christians created a Jesus who was just the opposite. So afraid of human feeling and emotion were the early Christians (they probably wanted their Messiah to appear more than human) that they stripped their Jesus down to an unemotional, joyless, humorless prophet for which there are few traces of any of the human qualities I consider among our most divine.

Such a Jesus would have been impossible: To be human is to know joy, passion, and ecstasy. I wish it could have come from the lips of Jesus (and maybe it did!), but there's a Jewish proverb that states: Whatever legitimate pleasure we deny ourselves on earth will also be denied us in heaven. If we deny ourselves the joy of life, the joy of the spirit, when we don't allow our own spirit to touch and direct us, then we are denying ourselves heaven on earth. For where we stand is a gate of heaven; we are assembled on holy ground. God is in this place—which is to say, joy is here, ecstasy can be ours.

Life

Nature, the Cosmos—let's call it Life with a capital "L"—is prejudiced toward a balance or harmony which It determines. Because we a part of that process, we also can flourish. In this sense then, there is Life outside of ourselves, and yet we—and other creatures—are all a part of this life, as in an interdependent web: we are the interdependent web in the same way that Life is.

Life is good because Life keeps us living: Life is good because it is the meaning of living. We don't study it to have meaning, we live it, we dance meaning into life, we embrace living into meaning. Life is not a problem to be solved, life is a mystery to be lived, to be lived in harmony and balance with the rest of the world, to be lived with an open mind and a tender heart. The meaning is in the mystery, but this is so difficult to understand.

An American tourist found himself in India on the day of the pilgrimage to the top of a sacred mountain. Thousands of people would climb the steep path to the mountaintop. The tourist, who had been jogging and doing vigorous exercise and thought he was in good shape, decided to join in and share the experience. After twenty minutes, he was out of breath and could hardly climb another step, while women carrying babies, and frail old men with canes, moved easily past him. "I don't understand it," he said to an Indian companion, "How can those people do it when I can't?" His friend answered, "It is because you have the typical American habit of seeing everything as a test. You see the mountain as your

enemy and you set out to defeat it. So, naturally, the mountain fights back and it is stronger than you are. We do not
see the mountain as our enemy to be conquered. The purpose of our climb is to become one with the mountain and so
it lifts us up and carries us along. (told by Harold Kushner
in *When All You've Ever Wanted Isn't Enough*)

Learning how to walk on the earth, learning how to see
life, learning that life is not a problem to be solved but a mystery to be lived—this is the way to meaning. There is a
rhythm to Life, to the Cosmos. There is nothing new about
this—people have been learning and experiencing this for
millennia. But for us, children of the Puritans, of the Enlightenment, we shrugged off mystery, faith, and metaphor
and replaced them with knowledge, empiricism, and literal-
ism. And we struggle, as if getting up to dance only to discover
that our ankles have been tied together or our ears have been
stopped up: we are not free to move nor can we hear the
music, and so dancing is difficult, we are handicapped. And
we struggle, trying to make sense, to find meaning, to life.

Florida Scott-Maxwell brings many of my loose ends
together:

> Life is a tragic mystery. We are pierced and driven by
> laws we only half understand, we find that the lesson we
> learn again and again is that of accepting heroic helpless-
> ness. Some uncomprehended law holds us at a point of con-
> tradiction where we have no choice, where we do not like
> that which we love, where good and bad are inseparable
> partners impossible to tell apart, and where we—heart-
> broken and ecstatic, can only resolve the conflict by blindly
> taking it into our hearts. This used to be called being in the
> hands of God. Has anyone any better words to describe it?
> *(The Measure of My Days)*

Day after day, we are in the hands of God, we are in
the womb of Life, we are interlaced in the web of all living creatures. Through living we will find meaning—so
experience Life, live Life, dance Life, and celebrate our
time together.

Lilies of the Field
(Matthew 6:19–34)

Here's a story that is attributed to the Buddha: A man came across a tiger in a field. The tiger gave chase and the man fled. He came upon a precipice, stumbled, and began to fall. Then he reached out and caught hold of a little strawberry bush that was growing along the side of the precipice. There he hung for some minutes, suspended between the hungry tiger above and the deep chasm below, where he was soon going to meet his death.

Suddenly he spied a luscious strawberry growing on the bush. Grasping the bush with one hand, he plucked the strawberry with the other and put it into his mouth. Never in his life had a strawberry tasted so sweet!

There was nothing unusual about this strawberry—the likelihood is that it was just like any other. In fact, the man had probably had better strawberries. But the circumstances were unlike anything he'd encountered in his life, giving the piece of fruit a taste he'd never experienced.

In moments when we have been under pressure, uncomfortable, ill, or in great pain, life can be seen in a whole new way that prior to that point we just never realized; it never grabbed us like we now see it. Like the man caught between the tiger and the chasm, now life is strawberry-sweet! Now you know, you may tell yourself, so now things will be different. Or in the words of former UCLA basketball coach John Wooden: "It's what you know after you know it all that counts." How many times I have talked

with folks who, after an illness, crisis, or personal transformation, have sworn that they now have what counts—
perspective, a new meaning to life, the feeling that things
will be different. No more sweating the small stuff, the details. No more wasting time and life. Perhaps you too have
echoed these sentiments. And even though many, if not
most, of those who have sworn themselves to a new way
eventually go back to the old one, they really did have the
best of hopes: when they said what they did about not
sweating the small stuff, they really meant it.

While there seems to be this consensus about not
wasting life in the details, we all do it, don't we? I don't
know anyone who doesn't spend some part of their wak-
ing hours busy in what I'd call the small stuff. Beatle John
Lennon once said something like: "Life is what happens
while we're busy planning [for it]." We all have to plan,
and if the details or small stuff is in the planning, then a
good deal of life *is* in the details, life *is* the small stuff, the
stuff of worries and anxieties, problems and difficulties.

Then there are those who simply don't appear to get
caught up in the details—maybe it would be more accurate to say they simply accept the details for what they
are. I've read that Jacques Cousteau, named at age 82 the
most popular person in France for the fifth consecutive
year, has few regrets. Asked by a reporter what he would
have done differently in his life, the undersea explorer
replied: "I'll answer with a story my father told me. One
day he was invited to England to celebrate a woman's
115th birthday. He was welcomed by an old lady in an
armchair holding a glass of cognac and a cigar. A journal-
ist asked her the same question, and she answered, with
a delicious British accent: 'Oh, [I would do] the same
thing, but more often!'" (told by Dick Gilbert)

I've read this Cousteau piece a dozen times: That's the
way I want to go, and my guess is that others find it pretty
appealing—no regrets, not even the small stuff. In fact,
the woman seems to be saying, bring me some more, bring
on life. What a great attitude!

So what's stopping us? William Maxwell frames the question like this:

> The great, universal problem is how to be always on a journey and yet see what you would see if it were only possible for you to stay home: a black cat in a garden, moving through iris blades behind a lilac bush. How to keep sufficiently detached and quiet inside so that when the cat in one spring reaches the top of the garden wall . . . you will see and remember it, and not be absorbed at the moment in the dryness of your hands. (*New York Review of Books*)

I often wonder if we haven't been set up for dissatisfaction. We so easily focus on the big stuff and let it define whether or not we're successful. Given who we are, the kinds of backgrounds that most of have come from, given our faith and educational history, we are not, as a community of individuals, short on motivation, drive, or accomplishment. So, is there an end to our (my) appetite for success, notoriety, and victory? Phyllis Theroux talks about this in *California and Other States of Grace:*

> I wonder now, whether accomplishments / Have any real significance as the world defines them. / I suppose they do, or at least we're inwardly urged / To create things to prove that we / Were around for a few years. / But, beneath the books, music scores / And brilliant conceptions we foist upon the world, / Perhaps our real accomplishments lie elsewhere. . . . / In a conversation we can't remember having, / A small relationship that gets someone else believing / In something more powerful than self-doubt.

Theroux is making an effort to remind us that there is satisfaction and meaning in what at first glance might appear as the details, that there is value in the small stuff.

In the Gospel of Matthew, chapter 6, the "lilies of the field" piece has always been a favorite of mine. Keep in mind that this is just a small part of a huge section of teachings that Jesus is giving that begins with what we recognize as "The Sermon on the Mount," and then continues with strong combinations of common sense and inspiration, comfort and support.

His audience is probably lower- and lower-middle-class folks who are followers of Judaism, a religion which at the time is extremely structured and legalistic: these people had a rule for everything and a person to consult for every question you could fathom! Unitarian Universalism couldn't get any further from this form of orthodoxy. Yet I think we can relate to the context in this way: the kinds of expectations, constraints, and assumptions that we all must live with are not that different from those of Jesus' listeners. While they aren't of a religious and theological nature, the effect is the same. Just as people then were overwhelmed with faith details and religious particulars that had their heads spinning and forcing them to wonder what the purpose of it all was, so are we often overcome with particulars and details that throw out of balance any sense of purpose and meaning we thought we had.

Then, along comes this Jesus who, like them, is a practicing Jew, a teacher. The gospel tells us that he says to the crowd (and I'm paraphrasing), Look, quit worrying so much about whether or not you're doing everything the right way. Have a little faith and trust. Believe that the same power (God) that has given you life and takes care of all living things will also take care of you. But, he reminds them, don't be stupid about it. Don't make more trouble for yourself than you have to. Listen to your heart, your conscience, and do what is good. Don't try to be what you are not. Take care of yourself, don't overdo it. Just try to lead a good life, and you'll be OK.

Go back to Matthew 6, read 19–34, and I think you'll come out in the same place I have. Jesus isn't telling them to simply throw all caution to the wind, to simply believe in God and expect everything to be OK. Pay attention to your life is what he's saying, pay attention to all of life. Embrace your living, day by day, live each day to its fullest: "So do not worry about tomorrow, for tomorrow will bring worries of its own. Today's trouble is enough for today." (v. 34)

That's pretty sound advice no matter who said it. Whether it's the small stuff or the big stuff, it's all life—living is in both and there's plenty of each for us all. What it really comes down to is engagement, being fully present to life, all the time. I know that's hard—I don't claim to be able to do it. But at the very least, or perhaps at my best, I would like to be able to say what Mary Oliver claims at the end of her poem "When Death Comes":

> When it's over, I want to say: all my life / I was a bride married to amazement. / I was the bridegroom, taking the world into my arms. / When it's over, I don't want to wonder / if I have made of my life something particular, and real. / I don't want to find myself sighing and frightened or full of argument. / I don't want to end up simply having visited this world.

In its details and enthusiasms, in its pain and victories, in life's small stuff and satisfactions, let none of us be a visitor.

Meaning

Each of us, probably every day, has countless turning points which we aren't even aware of, we don't even know they happen—we simply move ahead. Occasionally, always in retrospect, we might look back and isolate a turning point, maybe even a couple, and wonder "what if," or "why."

We all do this, this looking back and wondering. In fact, some obsess about it while others aren't so ritualistic or compelled, and still others just give occasional attention to these past turning points. But we all do it because these turning points are often looked at as meaningful—in large or small ways they have changed the course of a life, usually our lives.

We do it because we are meaning-making creatures—meaning-making is as essential to our being as are breathing and eating. I don't know if there is a meaning-making gene that we're born with, but I wouldn't be surprised if they found one (or several!). We seek answers as to "Why?" and "How come?" and all their countless variations. We'll even go back over a week, a year, a lifetime looking for meaningful turning points—great and small.

Virtually everywhere we go, we can see the tensions and challenges of meaning-making being acted out—at the movies, in classrooms, in the halls of Congress, home life, competitive athletics—just about everywhere you find the search for meaning. And of course, it's at the root of religion—meaning-making is what religion is all about.

Every religion has a particular way of meaning-making that is unique, it's their own path. If you personalize this path it's called faith. Whether or not it would be completely accurate, I would bet that most of you could say something about every religion in the world and/or it's denomination and why it's different from another—for the purpose of this exercise it wouldn't make any difference whether your view came from experience, reading, or hearsay. Because after such a sharing and maybe some discussion, it would become clear that every faith tradition has its own corner on the meaning-making process. We're all looking for meaning, and there are many, many ways to go and get it, shape it, understand it.

Messiah

The Messiah, according to scriptural history and theology, is the King of the Jews, ordained and sent by God as a deliverer. The arrival of the Messiah will inaugurate a new beginning, life as never known before, and God's chosen people will finally be saved. The New Testament tells us that the Messiah has come—that Jesus, the Son of God, is the Messiah and came to deliver not just the Jews, but all who choose to believe. This was but the first coming, a warning wherein he suggested how we might order our lives so that when he comes again—the Second Coming—we will be ready when he ushers in a new age, the Kingdom of God. As you can imagine, this was not and is not a popular message among Jews; it challenges and displaces a central theme in their belief system: they believe that the Messiah has yet to come the first (and only) time.

But let's not stop here. Messiah is also any religious deliverer or liberator, and so we could include Mohammed, the final prophet who for followers of Islam is their link to God, salvation, and new life. For a Muslim, Judaism and Christianity are but recognized subplots in the conclusive distillation given to Mohammed.

There's something about all of this messiah belief I always intuitively knew but was never able to vocalize until I read this passage in *The Search for God at Harvard:*

> In my world religions class, Professor Eck related . . . the [Hindu] idea of the "manyness" of God. It is an alien idea

not only to the Western religious imagination but to our entire cultural construct. All of modern Western thought could be said to be grounded in monotheism. We all believe in only One Truth. In our minds, there is only one Cadillac, one president, one cola ("the Real Thing"), one Harvard.

One Truth. That's what the messiah represents: one way, God's way, we are told, the only way, monotheism and monomessiahship. This Western religious concept has been so ingrained in us that it permeates everything of significance, everything that is religious, that we think about and do. When it comes to the pushing-and-shoving issues in our lives, to what really makes us who we are and what we want to be, how often we become "mono" focused, messiah-focused. What is it that will finally provide the turning point? Who is it that will finally make the difference? What's going to happen that will inaugurate my better days? Who's going to "save" me, nurture me, mold me, show me? When will all of this finally happen? Where is my messiah? How long must I wait?

At some level, consciously or not, many are waiting on the messiah. And furthermore, all of the major religious traditions, both Eastern and Western, are wrong and they are right: the messiah has not come, the messiah will not come, and yet, the messiah has arrived and has gone and still is among us. Perhaps this is the "manyness" of God.

I don't think it would be a misstatement or misrepresentation to interpret all of Western religion's messiah messages as boiling down to this: "Work on your attitude." None of them—neither Moses, Jesus, nor Mohammed— is suggesting that we postpone living, that is, wait for something better. They all are telling us to get on with life, to live. Messiahs in this sense can provoke zest for life, an impatience for living.

Don Harrington at Community Church in Manhattan told of a Sunday when he was speaking about the messiah. And as he spoke, a man with long white hair flowing down around his long white beard came shuffling down the center isle. Don saw him coming, but wasn't sure what was going to happen. The prophet-looking man crossed in front of Don, and made his way to the stage stairs and started up toward the pulpit saying: "It's all right, I'm here, I'm here." Don quickly responded with "Not yet, not yet." The man stopped and queried: "Not yet?" And Don repeated, "No, not yet!" To which the old gentleman responded, "Oh. OK, not yet." And shuffled his way back to where he'd started.

So might be our response to the coming of a messiah: Not yet! we should shout to such an idea. "However mean your life is," says Thoreau, "meet it and live it; do not shun it and call it hard names." Waiting on the messiah is not a very positive attitude, an attitude that embraces living for now. Setting aside our messiahs, saying "not yet," gives us an opportunity to make life worth living, it provokes us to reconsider our attitudes for living; we have, as Thoreau asserts, an opportunity to meet life and live it.

And maybe in that reconsideration is something that has been suggested over the generations and written about by many, including Eli Wiesel. He tells of a Rabbi Zusia who before he died said: "When I shall face the celestial tribunal, I shall not be asked why I was not Abraham, Jacob, or Moses. I shall be asked why I was not Zusia." Wiesel concludes: "In every person there is something of the Messiah."

We know that it's so easy to look elsewhere; the whole idea of the messiah is that it comes from outside with no control by us. How terrifying, how frightening, how sobering the thought that we each could be our messiah: that we must depend on ourselves for transformation, that within ourselves is where we must turn for strength, that it's here where we have to look for our reason for waiting. Now I know that it's not completely a matter of just us. It's very Western, like monotheism and monomessiahship, to believe in ourselves, to turn inward for direction and sustenance, to look to our inner messiah. And this is OK, some of the time. But we also need to be aware of what's around us, because sometimes we miss the boat, we don't hear the message, we don't feel the stirring in the air of something near. We've got to pay attention to what comes close by, not be so focused on our own self that we miss all the action. It may not be so intelligible at first, but don't dismiss it, it could be your ticket to living life fully.

A central theme of the messiah, a theme that runs throughout all of the great religions (with or without a messiah), is learning to live in and trust the here and now. We don't have to be waiting on whatever we think our messiah is going to bring, inaugurate, or transform. It's all here right now; we don't even have to wait for it—it's called living and it's going on even as we read.

I once heard someone call it "living in the present tense." Of course we are shaped by our past, sometimes for generations. And it would be foolish to never give thought to our future—we would only make our lives miserable, and those of generations. Yet from everything I've been able to observe, not enough of life is lived right now, and so I ask myself, what am I waiting for? All that the messiah promises is here for the taking. Ann Morrow Lindbergh describes it: "We find again some of the joy in the now, some of the peace in the here, some of the love in me and thee which go to make up the kingdom of heaven on earth." (*Gift from the Sea*) No messiahs, no waiting—just me and thee.

Whether it be a messiah to come, perhaps the Messiah Jesus, maybe a messenger from God like Mohammed, or a messiah by a hundred other names—the waiting for this messiah can put an end to living, because waiting for the messiah can be an end run around life and what makes living sweet.

Waiting on the messiah is not any fun, neither is it very satisfying nor fulfilling. We don't need to wait for the messiah—we still have our keys, keys that will open up many, many doors. The messiah is coming, you say? Long live the messiah? Maybe we should be shouting and singing, "Not yet, not yet!"

Miracles

People have always wanted answers to things they didn't understand, which could be one of the reasons for miracles. Miracles too are explanations, explanations for things that happen that we don't understand. We don't have any reason for why they happen so we go outside the usual explanations and answers—that is, outside the laws of the universe—and say that they were miracles. One person has said that a miracle is when something is more than the sum of its parts, as when $1 + 1 + 1$ equals more than 3. But today, we seem to make $1 + 1 + 1$ equal 3 virtually all of the time, making the likelihood of miracles awfully slim. We've become so good with answers—we have an answer for just about everything, or at least we're working on it. In other words, there's not much room for miracles.

Yet, it depends on whom you talk with. Let me give you some examples. One night when I was walking our company to their car, something caught my eye: it was the moon, a big, full moon. It took my breath away and for an instant it had a miracle-like quality to it, as if I was seeing it for the first time. How did it get there, why was it that particular color, why was it full? I knew none of the answers. But an astronomer or geologist might; they could answer all my questions and tell me more than I'd ever need to know about the moon on that Friday night. For them, there's nothing miraculous there—it was just another full moon.

Then there's something that we all have in common that I hear many people describe as miraculous. Do you know what that is? We were all born! To hear some describe the birthing process, it's a miracle. Yet, to talk with a doctor or physiologist, there's nothing unusual about birth. They can give you all the answers as to why and how it happens. It all makes perfect sense, to them.

Or what about some of the holidays we observe? For Christians, Easter celebrates the resurrection of Jesus Christ, the main event of the Christian religion. For Jews, the spring brings Passover, an outstanding event in the life of Judaism. For pagans and worshippers of Nature, spring celebrates the warm winds and rebirth of earth. Are these miracles? For many, they most certainly are. Yet others can give you answers—explanations—for all three. There's nothing miraculous about them at all.

So, what do you make of this miracle business? Do you believe in miracles? After all, some would say that anything that happens, anything we see or hear, can't be a miracle by the very fact that it happened, which means that it had to be subject to the laws of nature. The fact that it exists, that it happened, proves it wasn't a miracle! In other words, if it was outside the laws of nature, it wouldn't have happened! 1 + 1 + 1 will equal 3 every time.

But I'm not willing to give up on this so quickly. If there are no miracles, then how do you explain what appears to be miraculous? Or what about all those people who say they believe in miracles? Is it ignorance, simply not knowing?

I think it's two things: it's individual understanding and it's semantics, the meaning of the words we use. Let me illustrate both of these points with a story that I'm sure you may have heard. It's about a Unitarian Universalist minister who was living in an area that had been overrun with heavy rains and flooding. So bad had it become that, after failing to get out of the house, she had to wait to be saved. But she believed in God, and she knew after praying on this matter, her God would come to save her. Well, the floodwaters kept rising so she moved to the second floor. And outside her window, she saw a canoe come by. In it were some of the folks from her congregation and they yelled for her to come with them. "No, you go ahead. My God is going to save me." The waters kept rising, and soon she had to move to the attic. She heard a powerboat outside the window and it was the president of her congregation who encouraged her to get in. "That's OK, really. My God has a plan for me. Go on ahead." Well, she finally had to move to the roof because the waters had gotten so high. A helicopter came up and hovered and they yelled over the speaker that they were going to drop a line and she must take hold of it and be pulled to safety. She waved them off, shouting: "Help someone else. My faith is strong and God will rescue me." Well, she drowned. When she got to heaven and met her God she was angry. "What's the big idea? You told me you were going to rescue me, save me. Why did you fail and let me die?" And God replied: "Fail you? Fail you!! First I sent a canoe, then a boat. I even sent the helicopter. But no, you refused. What did you expect, a miracle?!"

What this story suggests to me is we all have different ways of "seeing." Some look at an object, event, or person and that's all they see. Others look at the same thing and see more. I think that this is what Einstein meant when he said: "There are two ways to live your life. One is as though nothing is a miracle. The other is as though everything is a miracle." I don't think Einstein was really talking about things that defy the laws of nature. I think he was talking about wonder—either you can live as though nothing is wonder-full or as if everything is full of wonder.

You may not believe in miracles, but you can believe and know wonder: the moon on a clear night, the birth of a living creature, the story of Jesus' resurrection, the saving story of Passover, the rebirth of spring, the love and friendship of another. These and much more are all wonders that any person can have—wonder-filled events.

Pagan

In her landmark study, *Bringing Down the Moon,* Margot Adler uses this definition of Pagan: "I use the word Pagan to mean a member of a polytheistic nature religion such as the ancient Greek, Roman, or Egyptian religions, or, in anthropological terms, a member of one of the indigenous folk and tribal religions all over the world."

There is a growing interest in and movement toward Neopaganism. In Adler's book, Isaac Bonewits comments that Neopaganism "concentrates upon an attempt to retain the humanistic, ecological, and creative aspects of these old belief systems while discarding their occasional brutal or repressive developments. . . ." Adler says that there are at least six reasons why people are choosing to call themselves Neopagans, at least in name:

First, their religious quest seeks the involvement of beauty, vision, and imagination. Often, poetry, drama, fantasy, and art were not to be found in mainline, accepted religions, at least not to the degree they wished. Especially in Neopagan rituals can there be heavy use of what many find missing in commonly accepted faiths.

Second, the Neopagans Adler interviewed tended toward intellectual interests, spending a great deal of time pursuing the fulfillment of their curiosities. In some parts of society this kind of pursuit is not only discouraged, but unacceptable. Many found themselves drawn to Neopaganism because it allowed for their interest in the far-out, the socially eccentric, the heretical, the unexplained.

Third, most Neopagans are searchers—they don't appear to believe in any one particular way of achieving meaning and satisfaction in life. In other words, they believe in an eclectic approach to fulfilling their religious needs.

Fourth, many women found the central attraction to Neopaganism was its support of feminism. For at least several thousand years (one could argue since the beginning of Christianity), women have longed for a religious tradition that supported them as women. Modern, western society has been dominated by patriarchal, nonegalitarian religions. Neopaganism lends strong support to both matriarchal and egalitarian religious thought and expression.

Fifth, as was the case for Adler herself, Neopaganism supports those who seek a religious response to the planetary environmental crisis. Nearly all of the Pagan traditions stress reverence for and harmony with nature, a principle only now being seriously considered by some Christian theologians, though it still meets resistance.

Finally, freedom. Neopaganism provides the freedom to participate in religious expression without having to go through a bureaucracy, however small and unassuming it might be—no ministers, no institutions, no hierarchy, no set rules about who can and who can't, no sin, and no guilt. In Neopaganism, there is a tremendous amount of freedom for its followers.

When I read all of these reasons, what did I hear? I heard that there is a religious and spiritual search by a growing number of people who have felt disenfranchised and let down by traditionally accepted religious faith. And I saw that the timing is right for an interest in a religion that supports mythological insight and satisfaction as well as ecological concern and interest. These appear to be high among the priorities of the Neopagan movement; they are needs that many are experiencing, needs currently being unfulfilled elsewhere.

I was intrigued and pleased to see that at one Unitarian Universalist gathering Harvard theologian Harvey Cox spoke about Paganism. Cox began by saying that he thought, given the current debates in theology in addition

to the sociopolitical climate of the world, that the Neopagan movement had a great deal to offer all people—it
was, he said, a refreshing development. Different from
what I had read or heard about earlier, Cox broke the pa-
ganistic response into three forms.

First, there are the retrievalists, those who seek to re-
claim the past. He suggested, howeer. that not only is the
evidence for what some seek very scanty, but why on earth
would anyone want to bring back antiquated concepts, beliefs, and practices that are oppressive for both women
and men? This would not be an improvement over some
of what is here today, simply a different form, replacing
one ignorance with another.

Second are the archetypalists. They seek out and hold
up the eternal images that have been in humanity since
the beginning of civilization. These archetypes, as Jung
suggested, are not found in history, but in ourselves, they
can be found in every culture and every generation. Unfortunately, says Cox, the archetypes that some Pagans
are pointing to are not so passive, loving, or nurturing.
Again, who needs archetypes that are destructive toward
people? We seem to have enough of this without recapturing the past.

Finally, there are the creative myth-makers, those
who seek a role for imagination in nurturing bold new
myth-making, myths built out of the old. Cox felt that
those following this path are to be applauded: it is by far
the most difficult way, but has the greatest reward. The
retrievalists and the archetypalists, as suggested, are
simply hanging on to the past. If the Neopagan movement
is really going to go anywhere, it has to break new ground,
it must begin by creating new myths from the old.

My guess is that there is a little bit of Pagan in us all.
And probably just in time, for as our world diversifies in
ways that will challenge our understanding of and commitment to pluralism, and as we continue to walk on the edge
of an ecological holocaust, we all could stand to be nudged if
not pushed out of the social and theological crevices and
ditches that we may have occupied for too long.

Pantheism

The summer of my junior year in high school I was selected to attended a highly acclaimed leadership camp on the shores of Lake Michigan. Each day of that week consisted of morning meetings, projects, some late afternoon and evening free time, and always at least one meeting with my counselor. The final morning was my evaluation: I was to meet with my counselor for an hour, at which time he was supposed to talk with me about the gifts I brought to leadership as well as the challenges I faced. That final Saturday we met for about 30 minutes and then, quite abruptly, my counselor asked me what God's plan was for me. I was completely caught by surprise—I didn't know what to say.

Though I had been a churchgoer all my life, raised in a good Christian family, and even though the seed had been planted years before about making the professional ministry my life work (which my counselor didn't know), I couldn't recall ever having talked with or heard from God. "Then right now," he told me, "right now I want you to go off down the hiking trail, find a place to be alone, and don't come back until God reveals His plan for you." Who was I to be contrary? I left the cabin, wandered through the woods until I found an isolated resting place, and there I sat wondering what to expect—actually, I was a bit frightened that something might happen! I mean, what would I do if God really did speak to me? After all, that's why I was there.

So there I sat, and sat, and sat. I watched the insects, watched and listened to the birds, I could hear the waves from Lake Michigan at a distance, I could hear and see the wind at the top of the of tall pines that surrounded me. But not once did I hear a word from the God I had been told would reveal my future plan. Finally, after what seemed like forever, I knew I had to go back—I had to prepare to leave. I would simply have to fabricate something to tell my counselor so on my walk back I rehearsed several conversations that sounded plausible. But when I arrived at my cabin, there was no one—later I was told that my counselor had left, he'd taken the early bus home!

That summer high school experience was just one of several similar kinds of encounters that I've had with other people's ideas of what they believe is a religious experience—of who their God is, but not mine. As it turned out, God did show up that morning in Michigan—I just didn't have the words to explain it, or the right frame of mind. I didn't allow myself the freedom to believe in a God I'd known all my life; I couldn't release myself from or get beyond the church and storybook images that had been ingrained in my brain (but fortunately not in my soul). In so many different ways, that experience and others are captured well in something Thich Nhat Hanh has said: "People usually consider walking on water or in thin air a miracle. But I think the real miracle is not to walk either on water or in thin air, but to walk on earth." (found in *Singing the Living Tradition*) As long as I can remember, my religion, theology, and spirituality have all been earth-centered, they have been rooted in everyday experience, in the world around me.

There is nothing new about this. What is new (or at least relatively new) is the fact that we've moved away from it, we've separated ourselves from Nature, from earth. For nearly all of humankind's existence, the sacred has been within reach, just below our feet, at the tips of our senses, within sight: Humankind was always at one with its world. But with the ages of reason and science, especially in the West, we have created dualisms and dichotomies: theologians, scientists, and philosophers have taught and convinced us that we are separate from other living things, that there is an order to the species and we're at the top, that humankind is not part of the earth but must be distinguished from it.

Speculation has it that when people began to separate and withdraw from the order that is Nature, when scholars, teachers, and leaders began to distinguish and elevate humankind from other living things, when theologians and clerics removed God from this world and placed Him in another world, there was an eroding chasm created that has ever since been causing dramatic and maybe irreparable harm and destruction to our physical, emotional, and spiritual well-being. These dichotomies are seen and experienced in the upheavals that have been running rampant through virtually every faith tradition; they are seen and experienced in the meaninglessness and existential crises that affect people who appear to have it all; they are seen and experienced in the senseless and thoughtless destruction of our environment. So separated have many become that they are adrift, they feel tied to nothing stable—many are rootless, with no bond to anything more enduring than their morning paper, no stability beyond the routine of their job, no security or comfort other than a few folks with whom they predictably spend their weekends.

It took decades to realize what I already knew, pushed by experiences like that morning in Michigan. It was in college that I finally understood and knew that my theology and religion—my outlook on life, what bound all of life together into a whole, what put it all together for me— was earth-based, rooted in Nature and nestled in the Cosmos. And now, looking back on where I've been, I'm almost embarrassed that it took me about forty years to finally affirm it and write about it. I say "affirm it" because to this day I still feel slightly uncomfortable revealing my earth-centered theology. I'm not sure why, though. Maybe because it's so simple—I mean, there is nothing very difficult or hard to learn or obscure or secretive about an earth-centered spirituality. It's there for everybody because we are all a part of it: we are the earth.

I call this way of thinking Cosmocentric theism, but it's really nothing more than pantheism, simply a version of what many today call Neopaganism. Unfortunately, Paganism—like other ancient words of our religious past—comes so full of negative connotations that to use that word immediately erects barriers so strong and high that I just try to avoid using it. Better to use Cosmocentric theism and keep people guessing!

My version of Paganism or pantheism or Cosmocentric theism goes like this: The Cosmos is everything that is: nature, the earth, the universe, and beyond. For all living things, the Cosmos is supportive—without it we die: it is quite literally our life-support system. Therefore, the Cosmos is sacred, the Cosmos is God, and God is the Cosmos. The two words are synonymous and interchangeable, but I prefer Cosmos because of the historical understanding that has distinguished God as separate from the earth, universe, and Cosmos. For me, God is Everything, the Cosmos is Everything—that's the extent of my pantheism since this word means God is all. There is an important distinction between this and saying that God is *in* the Cosmos, which is pan*en*theism. For me, that's just more dichotomies, separation—that's not putting it together. My theology, my faith is rooted in the belief that the Cosmos is God—that's pantheism. Consequently, everything of the Cosmos is sacred. And of course, because of this sacred quality, there are profound ethical and spiritual consequences for human behavior (and if you want to know more about this you can read my book *A Reason for Hope*).

At home I have a "spirit doll." It was carved by a tribesman who lives in New Guinea. I'm told that in his tribe, when a relative or loved one dies, a family member or friend is obligated to carve a likeness of the deceased, and while this is being done, the dead person's spirit is in the doll. The carving is completed out of respect, love, care, and concern not just for that dead person but for everyone who knew that person. It is a ritual and belief that has been carried out for a long, long time.

All of us, and maybe all living things—perhaps everything of the Cosmos—are like this spirit doll. We each have been blessed with the spirit of the Cosmos—or more traditionally if you like, with the spirit of God. We come from the Cosmos; we carry that spirit in us everywhere we go: from the moment we are birthed (and maybe before) until the moment we die (and maybe forever). Out of respect, love, care, and concern for not just ourselves but for every living thing, we must be gentle with this spirit. To do anything else would be not only foolish, but profane and sacrilegious.

Polytheism

Polytheism suggests that we reexamine and affirm the pluralistic nature of those things in life that we consider most meaningful. Put another way, why is it that I accept the idea that there can be only one source of meaning in my life? I've heard it said that monotheism is but imperialism in religion. Our daily and religious landscape is simply not that stagnant and narrow to accommodate only one source of ultimate meaning. Why is it that we feel as though what is good for us, what works for us on the outside—that is, multiple sources of meaning—isn't also good and of value for us in matters of religious belief?

Polytheism is an attitude and perspective that affects everything we do—it is a way to look at our life and the world. This is what Alice Walker is talking about in her essay "Oppressed Hair Puts a Ceiling on the Brain." She writes: "It was the way I related to it that was the problem." If we choose to believe that the universe, religion, Nature, or whatever else we consider to be most meaningful—of ultimate meaning—is to be considered and expressed in a limited, singular way, then so be it, the choice is ours. It's our perspective and attitude that have narrowed the field, the field itself hasn't narrowed. Near the end of her essay, Walker says: "My hair was one of those odd, amazing, unbelievable, stop-you-in-your-tracks creations—not unlike a zebra's stripes, an armadillo's ears, or the feet of the electric-blue-footed boobie—*that the Universe makes for no reason other than to express its own limitless imagination."* (emphasis mine) To date, I haven't heard of any significant limits on what the Universe can do and what it cannot do. Quite the contrary, it is *limitless* in what it comes up with. Polytheism attacks the notion that there is singular, ultimate meaning.

Prayer

Freeman Dyson, in *Disturbing the Universe,* tells a story of a scientist who from early morning to evening sat in his office, pounding away at his computer keyboard. Throughout the day, his office mate would look over his shoulder, but never did he ask any questions. Finally, going-home time arrived, and the scientist didn't budge. His partner could no longer contain himself and blurted out: "What are you doing?! All day long, you haven't moved. It's driving me nuts. Come on, it's time to leave." "I can't, I have to finish," was the response. "What are you writing?" his associate asked.

"Well," the exhausted scientist confided, "just in case I die during the night, I wanted to get everything down I know, just by chance that God might want to know the facts after I'm gone." His partner was in disbelief: "What? Is that what you've been doing? Don't you think God Almighty knows the facts?" To which his colleague replied, "Yes, yes, of course God knows the facts, but not *this version* of the facts!"

So it is, I believe, with most of Unitarian Universalist theology and practice. We are a faith tradition that thinks about and practices religion liberally—that is, with an open mind. We are free thinkers, unrestrained and unencumbered by creed and dogma. Consequently, I know of very few who wouldn't relish the idea, if given the opportunity, of telling the Almighty their version of the facts!

And what better way than by prayer. But then, is prayer? For us, giving a simple answer to this mig_____ like asking an Eskimo about snow. I've read that Eskimos have more than a dozen words for snow because it is an important part of their environment. And so it is with prayer, as with many other of the traditionally accepted customs in religion. People throw the word around, even asking for prayer, as if there's a common understanding of what it means, when really nothing could be further from the facts—facts for which there are many versions.

My experience with Unitarian Universalists has been that prayer is a turn-off because it's confusing, misunderstood, and in general has received a bad rap. Just as with other traditional religious customs, the typical religious liberal response often is to move as far away from the offending, misunderstood practice as possible—which actually isn't very liberal behavior at all, but rather is quite reactionary!

We want to do things right—who doesn't? That even includes praying. And if you were brought up the way I was, then you too were led to believe that there's a right way to pray and, by implication, a wrong way. It can be really easy to get caught up in the structure, the hows and whys and the to-whoms and for-whats. And if you think about it long enough, it all becomes very confusing and doesn't make much sense.

So, let's look at prayer as if we didn't know all of that stuff in our past. Or, if you find value in all or even pieces of that past, I hope I can prompt you to expand on your current understanding and practice. For awhile then, I'm going to walk around prayer. Imagine it in the center of a circle: I'm going to walk around it, view it from different perspectives and parts, and then having completed the circle, I'll jump in.

I like the way Greta Crosby framed the practice of prayer in *Tree and Jubliee*. She speaks about four contexts for prayer: conflict, sorrow, peace, and joy. That just about covers the range. In other words, prayer is good for any time.

She goes on to hold up three opportunities in these contexts. One is talking in quest, which is speaking while searching or speaking about the unknown, verbalizing the tension we feel from looking but not finding. Another is listening in silence. We all know that ours is a culture that must fill the void of silence; whether we're at home, in the car, or with a group, there's usually got to be something audible going on—music, the TV, a conversation. If there's a silence, fill it! But Crosby urges us to listen in silence to hear . . . what we'll hear. And third, she says prayer is for letting go of the little self. I'm going to guess that she means letting go of the self that gets caught up in the particular, principled, isolating events, issues, and values of a day. Prayer is an opportunity in conflict, sorrow, peace, or joy to see life in a larger way, to see life as a vision, living in connection instead of separation, gaining a sense of being tied to something other than what we can see and feel in our immediate circle of people and things.

And just what might that something be? After all, Unitarian Universalists are the ones who have been accused of praying "To whom it may concern," which some prefer to the other options. Again, we come into religion having been told, traditionally at least, that our prayer must be directed, have an end place—usually God.

But getting caught up in the particulars like selection and structure, the how-tos and to-whoms, becomes a distraction. My sense is that Unitarian Universalists have always had an inkling of these problems, which is one of the many reasons we remain creedless and dogma-free: these become yokes around our religious necks which harness the spirit in a theological oppression we neither seek nor desire. I recognize that this isn't for everyone.

I have a friend who is a practicing Catholic. He has also been Episcopal and Lutheran. He has an attraction to structure and ritual. I'm never quite sure if it's for my benefit or not, but whenever we talk about the church or theology, he's in utter disbelief that I don't have all the words, structures, and practices that so easily flow from his mouth in describing accepted orthodox belief. But to me that's all icing on the cake, it's the fluff, the dessert which supplements the meal—it's not the meal itself. We can learn all the right words, be familiar with the appropriate customs, know the styles, reasons, and methods, but if we begin from the wrong place, then all this other stuff doesn't mean anything at all. This story recorded in an eighteenth-century Hebrew book supports my point:

> A young man wanted to become a blacksmith. So he became an apprentice to a blacksmith, and learned all the necessary techniques of the trade: how to hold the tongs, how to lift the sledge, how to smite the anvil, even how to blow the fire with the bellows. Having finished his apprenticeship, he was chosen to be employed at the smithy of the royal palace. However, all his skill and knowledge in handling the tools were of no avail and his delight came to an end when he discovered that he had failed to learn to kindle the spark. (story told by Dick Gilbert)

So it is with prayer. Without the spark, without coming to prayer with the right motivation, attitude, or posture—which is all to say that your heart has to be in the right place—what meaning can there be to prayer?

In other words, you have to pray with a posture of openness. One person has called it innocence, and in this sense, he says, praying is not for the wise, but for the person who is willing to lay themselves open for what may come. Lily Tomlin pointed out one of the great ironies of prayer, of being open: "When we talk to God," she says, "we're praying. When God talks to us, we're schizonphrenic." (*The Search for Signs of Intelligence in the Universe*) Or another way to put it: you've got to be careful when you pray, because you may get an answer, and then what are you going to do!

This brings up the whole idea of what you "get" when you pray, of the purpose of praying. There are at least three (and you can add as many others as you might like):

Praying can be an opportunity for reminding ourselves (and those around us) to be grateful for food, friends, family, living—you fill in the blank. Quite often, it seems to me, I take an awful lot for granted, even during what feels like the worst of times. But even then, I can be grateful, though it's not easy to conjure up grateful thoughts at those times.

A second purpose is what Greta Crosby focused on: prayers give us insights into ourselves and possibly others. These are prayers that let us know about our limits. The great Jewish mystic Abraham Heschel wrote, "prayer clarifies our hopes and intentions. It helps us discover our true aspirations, the days we ignore, the longings we forget. It is an act of self-purification." (*The Wisdom of Heschel*)

And third, prayer connects us. If done in a group, like in church or around the dinner table, it ties us to the person speaking the prayer as well as the others listening. When we pray in private, we have a sense of being connected to whatever it is beyond us or in us that we need connecting with.

Life can be a prayer, but only if you maintain a sense of awareness of what's going on. If you blindly walk through your days and weeks, your relationships and private moments without giving them any thought, context, or grounding—any centering—then there won't be any sense of prayer to life. When you look at your life as a prayer, all of its events and people, when you hold these up for reflection and comment in a deliberate and focused kind of way, so that you're aware of what you're doing, then you're praying.

This isn't to say that the traditional prayers aren't of value. Of course there is a time and place for them. I'm called on to perform these quite often, for example when I'm the chaplain-on-call at the hospital. When someone there, who I usually don't know, asks for a specific prayer like the Lord's Prayer, that is not the time nor place to enter into theological discussion: it would be totally inappropriate, as would my telling them, "I'm sorry, I don't do those kinds of prayers." The reality I must accept and honor is that for some, there is meaning, comfort, and great personal value in structured and directed prayer. I can do this, and I can do it without difficulty.

But when I'm on my own, when I'm asked at a meeting or the dinner table to give a prayer, well, then that's very different. Then I feel I'm on my turf, I don't have to meet the expectations of others, I simply have to feel good about what I do. I can do nothing more than speak out of my own self. That's what prayer is: speaking from the depths. I may address my prayer to a conventional source, like God, and I may not—frankly this isn't always what's most important. What's of far greater value, what is the only rule or condition is that I say not what I think I ought to say, but what I want or need to say. This is speaking from my depths.

When it comes to prayer, honesty, sincerity, and simplicity go a long way. There have been times, for example, when I come home from the hospital wondering whether I've really screwed up. I was at the hospital, alone with a patient or even with the family. I was asked to pray, and I didn't want to pray, but I did. I always begin with unannounced silence and then I give it my best shot. But I have to feel OK with that—that's the best I can do. There's a wonderful Hasidic tale that makes my point:

Late one evening a poor farmer on his way back from the market found himself without his prayer book. The wheel of his cart had come off right in the middle of the woods and it distressed him that this day should pass without his having said his prayers. So this is the prayer he made: "I have done something very foolish, Lord. I came away from home this morning without my prayer book and my memory is such that I cannot recite a single prayer without it. So this is what I am doing to do: I shall recite the alphabet five times very slowly and you, to whom all prayers are known, can put the letters together to form the prayers I can't remember."

And the Lord said to his angels, "Of all the prayers I have heard today, this one was undoubtedly the best because it came from a heart that was simple and sincere."

He had the spark, a spark that caressed the essence of the moment, a moment to be addressed with simplicity, sincerity, and honesty. Anything less is not prayer. Prayer is speaking from your depths. Doing this, you won't go wrong.

Religion

What is a religion? What does it mean to be religious? Is Unitarian Universalism a religion, a denomination, a faith? When you choose to call yourself a Unitarian Universalist, are you making a claim to religion or simply acknowledging which church (or churches) you're staying away from?

In looking for answers to these questions I'm going to start out with a statement made by Jack Miles, author of *A Biography of God,* who wrote in the *New York Times Magazine:* "Religion has always been, among other things, a response to the intellectual inadequacy of the human species." Which is to say that we are question-asking and problem-solving creatures. When we are asking questions and solving problems—and this is being done for a great deal of our time—we are creating meaning. In this sense, we are meaning-making creatures too. And that's what religion seems to be all about: meaning-making. We humans thrive on meaning, and when it doesn't exist, we create it. And when we can't create it, when there is no meaning in our life, we get frustrated, shaken, angry, depressed, disillusioned, and unhappy. Religion, then, is the response to the feeling—happy, glad, sad, or mad—that arises from the gap (or lack of one) between expectation and experience: the expectation (or hope) of having meaning to life and the experience (or reality) of missing it.

"OK," you may be saying, "but what's religion? All you've told me is how religion happens, the process that results in the religious response. But what is a religion?" Religion is simply a set of beliefs that gives meaning to your life. The word *religion* comes from the same Latin root as does the word *ligament,* implying a binding or re-binding of things together. Religion is a set of beliefs that binds your life together, it holds your life in place; religion is the set of essential unifying beliefs (which is called a faith) that gives your life meanings that will either nar-row or close the gap between expectation and experience, providing for life purpose, direction, and definition.

Many choose from the tried-and-true selections of meanings available, the sets of beliefs that are called the world's religions. Each of these come with time-honored and time-tested versions of gap-closing measures, mean-ing-making beliefs that are followed by billions. And while the specific creeds, dogmas, and rituals vary tremen-dously, each of these religions, at its most fundamental level, is simply a response to the inadequacy of the hu-man intellect to resolve the dilemma between experience and expectation, closing the gap between what is and what could be.

One of the parts of my work that I enjoy the most is listening to people describe how they have come to terms with this gap, this inadequacy, which has resulted in their choosing to participate in the life of a church community. This often comes during one of the many classes I coordi-nate, where we sometimes begin with individuals saying something about their religious or spiritual journey— their childhood experiences, revelations, turning points, and how they came to Unitarian Universalism. In-evitably, and always in their own way, each person de-scribes how they have tried to close the gap, how they've tried to find meaning and definition to life. While each story is unique, there are always a lot of similarities. One of these similarities is the desire for both an understand-ing of religion as well as a satisfaction from it. Or to put it another way, to balance intellectual and spiritual/emo-tional needs. Or to put it still another way, to balance left and right sides of the brain. I have yet to hear a story that contradicts this; I have yet to know of a religious faith that doesn't struggle with this desire for balance.

The intellectual need seems to be met the most easily: it's met with theology. Theology literally means the study of God, but more broadly it's understood as a reflection on faith. Basically, theology is the logic behind a specific religious way. Every religious faith has a theology which tells the whys and hows of its beliefs, mainly for its followers, but of course theology is available to anyone to read and learn about. Traditionally, every religion's theology has tried to answer certain questions and issues: these are often the reasons for the gaping chasms that rob many of meaning and direction. Questions and issues like: What is death? What is life? Who's in charge? Is there an end and what will it look like? What are good and evil? What is knowledge? Are we alone? How these are answered can make you look either brilliant or like you just saw a Woody Allen movie (or both!).

Many confuse theology and religion: some think that a religion is its theology, which is why Martin Buber's comment is important. He suggested that the difference between religion and theology is the same as the difference between having dinner and reading the menu. Yes, religion will have theology: we all love to talk about religion. But let's not forget that religion begins as a response—a response of the heart, the soul, the spirit—religion begins with a feeling, an emotion, a recognition that something's not right or something's better than you'd imagined, or it begins with an "Aha! Now I see!" Religion starts with a visceral response and slowly moves its way to your intellect where that response is then analyzed and scrutinized, inspected and digested, and eventually framed in a suitably structured (and often compromising) way.

So, with all of this now under our belts: Is Unitarian Universalism a religion? The question deserves an answer (even though I don't like the question—and I asked it!). It's a question that others ask me, that maybe you've been asked. One of the comments I have heard hundreds of times is from members who say to me a version of: "I have this friend who would really like this sermon/service/program/church school/class, but they're religious and wouldn't fit in here."

I think I know what this means. It means that this person would like creeds, prayers, dogma, rituals, they would like all the traditional things that are usually associated with more orthodox worship experiences. And that's just fine; I know that our way of religion is not for everyone. But let's not suggest that we aren't religious. We are very religious people. What we do on a Sunday morning and during the week I consider to be very religious. In fact, that's what this church is all about: religion. Everything that goes on here, seven days a week, is about the response we're shaping to the awareness and acknowledgment of the gap between what is and what could be, between head and soul, between expectation and experience.

Historically, Unitarianism Universalism began as part of the Protestant Reformation—the break from the Roman Catholic Church (we were in the second wave which is called the Radical Reformation). We were Christian—liberal Christian. For our entire history, until just recently, we have been considered liberal Christian. As such, we were a Protestant denomination, a subcategory within Protestantism just like the Methodists, Presbyterians, Episcopalians, Quakers, etc., who are all Christian Protestant denominations. Yet as far as I can see, there have always been individual Unitarians and Universalists who have kept Christianity at arm's length.

I can't give an exact date (perhaps there isn't one), but around World War II, Unitarianism and Universalism began to move away, slowly at first, from Christian Protestantism. More and more of our members began to believe that the Christian way of religion, its dogma and rituals, was too limiting a response to the search for meaning. Former UUA president Bill Schulz says that a basic tenet of our open and free religion is "that the mysteries of creation are so great as to overwhelm every human attempt to capture them in a single channel of religious faith." (*Our*

Chosen Faith) Eventually, Protestantism didn't recognize Unitarian Universalism as part of its fold because we don't have a creed that affirms the divinity of Jesus Christ. So we are no longer a part of Christianity, even though our historical roots are clearly there, even though we have members who call themselves Christians. As a group, an association of congregations, we don't recognize a single person, scripture, or creed as determining, sacred, or essential to our way of religion.

So, yes we are a religion, the Unitarian Universalist way of religion whose theology is unitarian, its faith universalist, its worship creedless, and its polity congregational.* Like every religion, we have a unique way of ordering our lives together as a community called a church. We do this in response to the gap that calls out for meaning and definition, giving direction and purpose to life.

---

* See the essay on Unitarian Universalism.

Religious Experience

Harvey Cox reports that there is a favorite saying among Pentecostals: "The person with an experience is never at the mercy of the person with a doctrine." (*Fire from Heaven*) When I read that, not only did it speak to my sense of what is right, but it even sounded familiar.

Well, it should have sounded familiar! This idea of experience in religion is what I talk about in the first session of every class I teach on the basics of Unitarian Universalism: how Unitarian Universalists see faith through the lens of experience (rather than tradition, hierarchy, or sacred scripture). Each person's experience is the final authority when it comes to religious belief.

For Pentecostals, this is where they make the break from other religious groups, especially the fundamentalists, who believe in the inerrancy of the Bible. Of course, Pentecostals also read the Bible and believe it's the word of God. But they are not literalists, they are not fundamentalists who give all power and authority to sacred scripture. If the Holy Spirit speaks to them, then that experience far outweighs any church doctrine that demands unquestioning loyalty to scripture.

This means that Unitarian Universalists and Pentecostals share a powerful and quintessential notion of faith: In religious and spiritual matters, experience supercedes dogma. But how did they get where they are, and how did we end up where we are? You couldn't find two more extremely different approaches to the practice of religious faith, and yet we share this essential and profound belief that permeates everything else.

As a student intern at Community Church in New York City, one of my jobs was to be the chaplain to the UU students at Columbia and Barnard Colleges. The church gave me a lot of support in this by lining up our monthly speakers, which often included some very notable figures.

There were usually about ten to fifteen of us that would gather in an assigned room at the student religion center at Columbia, where most of the student organizations met. This one night, our guest speaker and discussion leader was Norman Cousins. What a night! There were just a few of us and we had this world-class thinker and writer all to ourselves for several hours.

Our discussion was wide-ranging, in-depth, thought-provoking, and very heady! It was everything that I loved about Unitarian Universalism. About halfway into the evening, from behind the wall in another room, we heard what sounded like dozens of people making noises, and, well, it sounded like what I associated with the noises a woman might make in the early stages of labor: grunts and groans, not too sustained, not clear enough to mean anything. And it kept getting louder and louder. Finally it reached a level of volume that made it hard for us to continue our discussion with Norman Cousins. It was the Columbia-Barnard Student Pentecostals, and they were speaking in tongues—they were filled with the Holy Spirit. Just as we were, they too were doing what they do best, they were sharing their good news.

We Unitarian Universalists and the Pentecostals were both speaking from experience, yet the results were dramatically different. Houston Smith characterizes the difference this way: When Bill Moyers interviewed him, Smith said that the Muslim Sufis speak of religious experience using the metaphor of fire. There are three ways to learn about and know fire. First, someone can tell you about it and you can listen. Second, you can see the fire yourself and learn about it by direct observance. Or third, you can be warmed or get burned by fire, experiencing it firsthand.

We Unitarian Universalists have become known, whether by scholars or laypeople, whether through research or jokes, for approaching the fire—religion—in the first two ways, both of which are passive, cerebral approaches. You could say that we think our way into and through religion. We are not known (regardless of whether this is accurate) for our direct religious experience, as the Pentecostals are. We are known as a way of religion that is cerebral, not experiential: We prefer to talk about the fire of religion rather than experience it.

What might we be experiencing? What is the fire that should warm us, that could burn us? What is there that we could share? Here is Frederick Buechner's accounting of his experience, of what he says is the fire in our lives:

> Several winters ago my wife and I and our twenty-one year old daughter went to that great tourist extravaganza near Orlando, Florida, called Sea World. There is a lot of hoopla to it—crowds of people, loud music, Mickey Mouse T-shirts and so on, but the main attraction makes it all worthwhile. It takes place in a huge tank of crystal clear, turquoise water with a platform projecting out into it from the far side and on the platform several pretty young women and handsome young men in bathing suits who run things. It was a gorgeous day when we were there, with bright Florida sunlight reflected in the shimmering water and a cloudless blue sky over our heads. The bleachers where we sat were packed.
>
> The way the show began was that at a given signal they released into the tank five or six killer whales, as we call them (it would be interesting to know what they call us) and no creatures under heaven could have looked less killerlike as they went racing around and around in circles. What with the dazzle of sky and sun, the beautiful young people on the platform, the soft southern air, and the crowds all around us watching the performance with a delight matched only by what seemed the delight of the performing whales, it was as if the whole creation—men and women and beasts and sun and water and earth and sky and, for all I know, God himself—was caught up in one great, jubilant dance of unimaginable beauty. And then, right in the

midst of it, I was astonished to find that my eyes were filled with tears.

When the show was over and I turned to my wife and daughter beside me to tell them what had happened, their answer was to say that there had been tears in their eyes. It wasn't until several years later that I happened to describe the incident at a seminar at the College of Preachers in Washington, and afterwards a man came up to me who turned out to be the dean of Salisbury Cathedral in England who asked me if I would take a look at part of a sermon he had preached a few weeks earlier. The passage he showed me was one that described how he had recently gone to a place called Sea World, and how he had seen an extraordinary spectacle there, in the midst of which he had suddenly discovered that his eyes were filled with tears.

My wife and I and our daughter and the dean of Salisbury Cathedral—I believe there is no mystery about why we shed tears. [You see,] the world is full of darkness, but what I think we caught sight of in that tourist trap in Orlando, of all places, was that at the heart of darkness—whoever would have believed it?—there is joy unimaginable. The world does bad things to us all, and we do bad things to the world and to each other and maybe most of all to ourselves, but in that dazzle of bright water as the glittering whales hurled themselves into the sun, I believe what we saw was that joy is what we belong to. Joy is home, and I believe the tears that came to our eyes were more than anything else homesick tears. God created us in joy and created us for joy, and in the long run not all the darkness there is in the world and in ourselves can separate us finally from that joy, because whatever else it means to say that God created us [with a divine spark], I think it means that even when we cannot believe, even when we feel most spiritually bankrupt and deserted, this mark [this spark] is deep within us. We have joy in our blood. (*The Longing for Home*)

Buechner's retelling of his experience is moving and disturbing. It's moving because I know he's right: joy is in our blood—the joy of living, of life—it's our essence; joy is at the root of religion. About this I have no doubt: I know it, I feel it, I've experienced it. What's disturbing about this is, how would we ever know? How would we, how would anyone, know from our Sunday mornings together that joy is at the root of our gathering? To look at Unitarian Universalists, to look at most of the mainline churches (with whom we are associated not only by heritage but by skin color), how could you tell that joy is in our blood? What's disturbing is that the joy is here, it's part of us, we can't get rid of it—it *is* in our blood. But where is it, why is it invisible, what happened? Why do we just think about joy and don't seem to show any outward expression or sign of it? I mean, if it's that much a part of us, and it's that powerful, how can we stand it? You'd think it would be right at the surface, just trying to bust out all over.

I believe there's a lesson to be learned in the story of an English doctor who was intrigued with Indian Hindus, who in their diet didn't eat enough vitamin B_{12} to keep a rabbit alive, yet never suffered from B_{12} deficiency. After trying to figure it out, he finally realized he'd have to go to India and observe it—maybe it was climate, the water, he didn't know but wanted to find out. When he was on site and had done just about everything he could do, he still couldn't come up with any explanation. Yes, their diet appeared to be totally void of B_{12}, and yet there were no problems related to a lack of it. He finally decided he needed to bring a Hindu into a controlled setting and study the issue more closely.

He got a volunteer whom he flew back to London. And there he fed him the same diet as he'd had at home in India. But this time, the Hindu developed a B_{12} deficiency! The doctor couldn't explain it. It turned out that the English food was too clean! Yes, it was the same food as the Hindu had eaten at home, but when the English prepared it, they'd washed away all the weevils and worms (and other critters) that had been in the fruits and vegetables, enough to prevent B_{12} deficiency. The English so sanitized their food that they'd robbed it of nutritive value for the Hindu. (Story found in Robert Johnson's *Ecstasy*)

I wonder if we've sanitized our religion, our time together on Sundays. I wonder if we've cleansed our lives of the joy that is as nutritive to religious and spiritual health and living as those critters were to the health and well-being of that Hindu. By becoming so cerebral have we robbed ourselves of the joy of experiencing the fire, the fire of a burning faith, a faith rooted in the joy of life?

Now, I want you to know that I'm probably being a bit unfair. I'm not trying to transform our congregations into the Pentecostal UU churches (though I must admit that this idea is intriguing!). I don't want anyone reading this to think I've said that Unitarian Universalists don't have spirit, don't have soul, don't know how to feel, can't be emotional, don't have rock 'em-sock 'em to their religious depth. Besides, is this all there is to religion? Is this what religion is?

I like the way colleague Dick Gilbert puts it: "Religion is more than mindless jumping up and down about how super it is to be alive." What he means by this is that sometimes life can be the pits, filled with setbacks, tragedy, and sorrow. To live means experiencing these valleys. It also means coming across plateaus—in fact, most of life can feel like one big plateau where not very much ever changes. Some might even say they prefer it this way.

Our religious and spiritual life must embrace all of these levels. If it doesn't, if it only has room for joy, then I think it's time to question the value of our faith. We need a faith for not just the mountaintops of joy, but the plateaus and valleys too. Ours must be a faith that recognizes all the experiences of living and says this is life too, these are aberrations. Ours must be a faith that embraces all human experience.

We're going to have our disappointments, setbacks— there will be times when maybe you're going to think that life has in some way broken its promise with you, the promise of fulfillment, satisfaction, or deep meaning, the promise of joy. This is going to happen; it's something every person could experience. And every person could also share that life gives us chances to start over—every day is an opportunity for renewal.

But we are the ones who must keep the promise of renewal alive. We and our Pentecostal brothers and sisters share this certain knowledge that religious faith is rooted in experience. But the Pentecostals appear to recapture their hearts every time they are together, they share in the joy that they know is their God, they're not waiting for the perfect, right time—now is that time! We might not choose to use their words, but we too share that experience. Everything we say is about acceptance, recapturing the heart, sharing our good news, renewal; these are the messages of our heritage, these are the messages, the good news, of our gospel still today.

We gather knowing it and feeling it too, but somewhere between the head and the heart and the sanctuary, it all may get detoured or lost or stymied, and it doesn't get shared with those who want and need to know about and experience the very same thing. How can we stand it?! What will finally move us to open up and share the experience of joy that we all know is ours, that we all are rooted in, that is in our blood?

Right Relations
(Doing unto Others)

There's a story told in the Talmud of a non-Jew asking the great sage Hillel, "Can you summarize all of Judaism for me while I stand on one foot?" And Hillel answered: "What you don't like, don't do to others. That's it; the rest is commentary. Now go study the commentary." (Told by Harold Kushner in *To Life!*) It's pretty clear that it's out of this tradition that Jesus tells many of his parables about relationships. It's from the Talmud that Jesus learned his ethics: "What you don't like, don't do to others." It makes sense to me—it's a wonderful sentiment. But we all know that not much is of lasting value in our lives if it isn't practiced, which is why Hillel doesn't stop with his summary statement; it's more than summaries, so "go study the commentary."

It we expect to enter into relationships that are going to make more kindness in our lives, if we wish to be treated well, if we want out of the hells we may live in, if we seek to create a better place in which to live and worship, then we must understand and practice what we want, what has come to be called right relations. Right relations is about putting people first, not rules and regulations, not all the commonly accepted ideas that might come from doctrine and tradition. Right relations means not doing to others what you wouldn't want done to you. It sounds so simple, it makes so much sense. Yet right relations is not how our lives have been organized.

Long before someone discovered that men are from Mars and women are from Venus, Carol Gilligan discovered the significance of right relations and the dramatic impact it has on the way we order our lives:

> Gilligan studied ethical decision making among adolescents and observed a distinctly different response in boys and girls. Boys more consistently described the ethical dilemma posed by Gilligan as a conflict between the values of property and life. Boys based their suggested action on what they considered to be the "right thing to do." In contrast, girls more frequently saw the same ethical dilemma not as a "math problem with humans," but as "a narrative of relationships." Girls based their suggestions for action on the value and quality of relationships and on "an awareness of connection between people" and on "the need for response." (Deborah Pope-Lance in *Creating Safe Congregations*)

Gilligan's work has helped us recognize that there needs to be a balance in the way we order our lives: "What was once a conversation about the relative merits of rights and rules must now consider the value of relationships." Getting it right means considering the value and importance of relationships in our lives—in the way we live.

But all of this is commentary: study it, and then do it, practice right relations. You can start just in the way you greet others; you can practice right relations with your family and friends; you can get it right at work or at school. Putting relationships first is full of opportunities, every day.

This isn't to be casually dismissed as soft theology, naivete, or wishful thinking. Right relationships make their impact in the most amazing ways. Just the other day I was at a meeting of colleagues and I think everyone there wondered if one particular minister would show up. You see, he had just been diagnosed with a terminal illness. Well, he was there and he asked to have a few minutes to talk with the group. He spoke for about 10 minutes and if I had to summarize what he said it would be this: Never, ever, underestimate the power, value, and meaningfulness of going out of your way to share your thoughts, prayers, a blessing, words of kindness with someone who is distressed. He mentioned all the times that he'd gone to visit people in the hospital or at homes, or counseled folks and concluded by saying, "I'll be thinking of you" or "I'll keep you in my thoughts and prayers." He confessed he was never really sure if it meant anything. But now he knew—it meant everything, at the end of a day it was often what kept him going.

His comments made me think of some lines from *A Raisin in the Sun*. Mama Lena admonishes Bernetha with: "Child, when do you think is the time to love somebody the most; when they done good and made things easy for everybody? Well then, you ain't through learning, because that ain't the time at all. It's when he's at his lowest and can't believe in himself 'cause the world done whipped him so." (Found in Don Wheat's *In Pursuit of Joy*)

Let's get it right—let's practice right relationships. "What you don't like, don't do to others." Be kind to others who are kind to you; be kind to others who aren't kind to you. "That's it; the rest is commentary. Now go study the commentary."

Sabbath

As a child, my Sundays were unique. Of course there was church, there was always church—no matter what!—and 90 percent of the time that was OK; I enjoyed the church of my childhood. But church was just part of Sunday. After church, there was always a family dinner, or sometimes we were invited over to somebody else's place; either way, Sunday dinner was special (which usually meant mashed potatoes and gravy!). And after dinner, we always did something as a family. Even if we did nothing, we did it together; that's just the way it was, there was never any question about it. And I just assumed that was the way everyone did it.

So, when I talk about Sundays being something, I have a built-in prejudice supported by positive recollections, which are in part rooted in the biblical story of creation where "the day of rest" originates. Here is how that story goes:

> And on the seventh day God finished the work he had done, and he rested on the seventh day from all the work that he had done. So God blessed the seventh day and hallowed it, because on it God rested from all the work that he had done in creation. (Gen. 2:2–3)

This is how the Sabbath day came about. In the book of Exodus, a day of rest becomes part of the covenant between God and the people of Israel:

> Six days shall work be done, but the seventh day is a Sabbath of solemn rest, holy to the Lord. . . . It is a sign

forever between me and the people of Israel that in six days
the Lord made heaven and earth, and on the seventh day
he rested, and was refreshed. (Exod. 31:15–17)

Of course, there have always been those who have chosen to ignore the Biblical story and covenant, reasoning
and responding in the same way a tailor did to a customer
who came in to pick up his pants: "Sorry, the pants aren't
ready yet. Next week." "What's taking you so long?" the
customer quipped, "God made the whole world in just six
days." "I know," the tailor said, "and look at the mess the
world is in and look at how good the pants are coming out."

Which is to say, not everyone has been a satisfied customer. It was Judaism that gave us the Sabbath, but it
was Christians who grew dissatisfied, mainly because it
was too Jewish. Seeking to distinguish themselves from
Jewish law and practice, Christians switched the Sabbath
from Saturday to Sunday—from the last day to the first
day of the week—while theologically explaining that it
symbolized not the creation story (from the Jewish book
of Genesis), but the resurrection story (from the Christian
Gospels). Remember that nearly all the early Christians
were Jews, which meant that you could make all these
changes on paper, but you were still left with figuring out
a way to enforce the change, because old traditions die
hard and this tradition was at least a couple of millennia
old—a big problem for the Christian hierarchy. (And of
course, the Sun's Day has its very ancient origins in pagan celebration. In this way, Christianity was at least a
third generation of faith dealing with this unique recognition.) We Unitarian Universalists have carried on with
the Christian Sunday and not the Jewish Sabbath—kind
of. To tell you the truth, I'm not sure we do either one very
well, which is too bad because I think there's something
there for us, something really important.

The whole idea of the Sabbath (and the Christian Sunday) is focused on not working, not doing what you do for
the other six days, creating a very special and unique spot
in the week. There are at least two historical reasons for

this. First, while the Israelites were in slavery, they had no choice but to work: they didn't own their bodies or their time, and were subject to their Egyptian masters. Having been enslaved, the idea of a day of rest was revolutionary and shocking to those around them.

And second, it's what God had done, what God had commanded Jews to do: to rest on the seventh day, which for Jews was Saturday, the last day of the week. To rest and praise God, by resting. The Sabbath begins at sundown on Friday and lasts until sundown on Saturday— 25 hours in which there is to be no work, and the more orthodox you are the more tightly drawn is the definition of no work.

In this spirit, here is a Sabbath prayer that Jews say:

> Lord of all creation, you have made us the masters of your world, to tend it, to serve it and to enjoy it. For six days we measure and we build, we count and carry the real and the imagined burdens of our task, the success we earn and the price we pay. On this, the Sabbath Day, give us rest.
>
> For six days, if we are weary or bruised by the world, if we think ourselves giants or cause others pain, there is never a moment to pause and know what we should really be. On this, the Sabbath Day, give us time.
>
> For six days we are torn between our private greed and the urgent needs of others, between the foolish noises in our ears and the silent prayer of our soul. On this, the Sabbath Day, give us understanding and peace.
>
> Help us, Lord, to carry these lessons of rest and time, of understanding and peace, into the six days that lie ahead, to bless us in the working days of our lives. (*Spiritual Simplicity*)

Rest, time, understanding and peace. These, then, are the shining stars of Sabbath, as they were for the newly liberated Jews from Egypt and as they are today. These were also to become the hopes and dreams of the Lord's Day, Sunday, for Christians.

But we all know that somewhere along the way, things went amok. It would be easy to point a finger at the

Christians of 321 who began tinkering with the Sabbath. But it would be just as easy and certainly more familiar to blame today's slow erosion of Sunday "blue laws" and the intrusion of weekend soccer games, meetings, homework, and e-commerce gadgets. For that matter, virtually everything that goes on during the week conspires to ensure that a "day of rest" is out of the question: I mean, who can afford a day of rest?

That's just the point of the Sabbath: we all can afford it, we all need it—it's time to consider it. Rest, time, understanding, and peace; renewal, perspective, bonding, and balance; reflection, connection, transcendence, and at-onement—it's these that I would guess every person might agree on, it's these that we find lacking in our lives, it's these that are tested and torn, abused and ignored, diminished and unreplenished weekly. Wordsworth said it this way: "The world is too much with us; late and soon, / Getting and spending, we lay waste our powers: / Little we see in Nature that is ours; / We have given our hearts away, a sordid boon!" It's a Sabbath—what Jews call Shabbat—that we need to work into our living. We all need a Shabbat, a Sabbath, a Sunday.

But it won't happen by itself. Nobody's going to come to you and tell you to rest for the 25 hours between sundown on Friday and Saturday or all Sunday or some other version of a Sabbath. The Sabbath may be there in Exodus 31, as part of the covenant, and it may have been decreed by Constantine in 321, and your parents and grandparents may have done it this way or that—but now, it's up to you. It's there for the taking, if you want it.

Your day of rest might include family, friends, and a thanksgiving for the intergenerational web of kinfolk who support and strengthen, nurture and feed your body and soul. You might wish to include an outstanding meal, listening to music, or a lively discussion; the pleasure of affection, rest, or a movie; a group walk, reading, or songfest. Let's call this celebration or receptivity, since, I would guess, we spend most of our week reacting and analyzing. Sabbath needs to make room for what Abraham

Heschel has called "radical amazement," the opportunity to simply look and see and feel what we may have been missing the other six days of the week.

As long as I'm suggesting that we all give serious consideration to incorporating a Sabbath into our lives, I also have a place where it could start, or at least a place that might be included in your Sabbath: church. After all, it's not called a sanctuary for nothing! Restoration, reflection, and celebration. I want to encourage you to think of Sunday morning as integral to your Sabbath (the beginning, the ending, or some part of it). I realize that the reasons you visit your congregation could be as many as there are people. I also know that restoration, reflection, and celebration can be found in different ways.

I love the story that Harold Kushner tells that makes my point. He recalls someone who once asked his father, "If you don't believe in God, why do you go to synagogue so regularly?" His father answered: "Jews go to synagogue for all sorts of reasons. My friend Garfinkle, who is Orthodox, goes to talk to God. I go to talk to Garfinkle." (*When Bad Things Happen to Good People*) Restoration, reflection, and celebration can be found in many different ways—the important thing is not to be dogmatic about how to find them, but to take advantage of the opportunities and possibilities that you are given.

My advice: don't let the Sabbath go to waste. Let's take Abraham Heschel's observation to heart: "As civilization advances, the sense of wonder declines. Such decline is an alarming symptom of our state of mind. Humankind will not perish for want of information; but only for want of appreciation." (*The Wisdom of Heschel*)

Appreciation. If there was one word that could describe Shabbat, the Sabbath, Sunday, that's it. What have you done to show your appreciation for life? You might want to consider Sunday a Sabbath.

Sacred Story

There are places and people that gave us stories—without stories, we are not complete persons. Judith Christ says: ". . . the meaning of our lives is revealed in the stories [we] tell, in [our] perception of the forces [we] contend with, in the choices [we make], in the feelings about what [we] did or did not do. In telling [our] stories [we] speak of parents, friends, lovers, ecstasy, and death—of moments when life's meaning seemed clear, or unfathomable. [We] reveal [our]selves in telling stories." (*Diving Deep and Surfacing*)

When I read this, I thought of all the hundreds, maybe thousands, of people I've met in "New U" classes, an introduction to Unitarian Universalism. In the first session, we always spend about an hour introducing ourselves and telling our stories; we tell about the religion or church of our childhood, our parent's religion, how we ended up here, and where we were in the between times; we talk about our searches, the detours and disappointments, the "ah-has" and "oh-nos." We talk about the difficulty of explaining what we believe, especially to others and most especially to family, who often don't quite understand this faith community—they often want to know what was wrong with the old story that worked for the litany of family members who can be named without much prompting at all!

We each have a story, a narrative, into which our life is set: it's our story. It's the way we talk about ourselves. As the years go by and a story is passed on from person to person, the cast and variables may change a bit, and perhaps even the point of the story may change. Still, it's our narrative, our story: it tells about what we value, what has shaped us, what gives our life meaning.

Myths are a special kind of story. Myths are sacred, fictional stories outside the time and place of history that tell about the fundamental meaning of human nature and life. Myths transcend a given people and place, and speak about all people at any time (even though they may use the characterizations and setting of the myth's origin). Myths can also be adapted to any time or setting and seemingly made that generation's own. Myths are remarkably flexible, while the kinds of characters and subjects may change. The great mythologist Joseph Campbell describes how certain sacred stories show up in tribes or societies from today back to the first civilizations of record, revealing that human beings' needs and meanings haven't changed in millennia.

All of this is to say what you already know or could have figured out: some stories are holy. These are the binding stories, the stories we tell ourselves or that we have chosen to make our own because they make sense of the pieces in our lives that don't seem to fit anywhere else. Take the major religious stories: they are holy, speaking of an original unity that their followers are trying to recreate or recapture, to replicate if only in a metaphoric way. Buddhism talks about the true Self; Taoism speaks of the Way; Judaism recalls the harmonious Creation; Christianity portrays oneness in Christ. For each there is a guiding story (of mythic size) that tells about a unity that is holy. For so many, this unity is stabilizing, life-giving, and is the cohesiveness—the peanut butter—of life in that it is there when all else appears to have failed. The words *holy* and *healthy* share the same root, which means "whole." The interdependency of these three—holy, healthy, whole—is claimed by many as a birthright; it's at the core of our being.

Sometimes, personal story (narrative) and religious myth (sacred story) become mingled, intertwined in such a way that separating them is difficult, even dangerous. You could probably tell about two or three examples of where and how you think (or know) this has happened: every decade, stretching back for thousands of years, has produced an example of a person or group that makes us call into question the health and wholeness of a holy story, regardless of who's telling it. Remember too that holy stories come in all shapes and sizes, and with all kinds of narrators and players. For example, some observers would say what we do on Sunday morning is but one more version of a well-rehearsed ritual and story that has been carried on, under many guises, since the beginning of time. In form and tradition we may share a common history with other faith communities and individuals, but in content and style the differences are dramatic and faith-shaping.

The professionals tell us that storytelling and interest in mythology have undergone a rebirth. This is not just a casual observation; we're talking about the value, meaning, importance, and vitality in the power of story and myth. I know this from direct experience because I'm a believer, I too understand, feel, and depend on the personal and sacred power and direction of story. And you know what else? I think each of us does. Make no mistake: the power and vitality of story are with us today for all the same reasons they were with our grandparents and as far back as the generations go. But there are at least two reasons why story, and in particular sacred story, is central for us today.

First, the world is doing a better job than ever of reminding us of how unconnected we are, of just how isolated we have become: often we sit in solitary speechlessness in the glow of our TV screen; we move around in the isolation of our autos; we hear about—and maybe we expect—every person's right to this or that with very little talk about what's good for community; and so many individuals have started down a spiritual path that has led them further and further away from any semblance of connection. I've heard it said that the last several decades could be characterized by the magazines we read: first there was *Time,* then *Life,* then came *People,* followed by *Us,* and finally *Self.* I'm waiting for the publication of *Id,* which seems to be the theme some have made their story. Narrower and narrower is the journey; how much more isolated and unconnected from each other have we become. And it's as though everything around us has conspired to support us in each step along the way as the bonds are severed to all the connections that other generations simply took for granted. Yet as all of this goes on, and even though we might willingly participate, I sense that many have grown weary if not suspect of those things that take us away from a sense of being grounded and rooted. People yearn to be connected to something larger than self.

Another reason why story, and in particular sacred story, is central for us is because the old stories aren't working. Ironically though, some of what we may think of as "old" stories are only several generations old, and in this sense they are quite modern. These are not mythic stories. (Actually many of the ancient stories, the myths, still do work!) These modern "old" stories which are not working include the stories of duality (in a world of diversity); the stories of fear and punishment (in a world of abundance); the stories of isolation and going it alone (in a world of the interdependent web); the stories of reason, education, logic, and science (in a world of irrationality and mystery).

So, the value and importance of story has returned— narratives and myths that give both comfort and depth, not only some explanation, but reason for being. They provide history and connection to the ages: narratives and myths give personal meaning and community solidarity not only for enlightenment, but for fun, because there is a spirited playfulness and vitality in so many of the stories which give our lives direction.

Saints

As part of my doctor of ministry work I was required to take a preaching class. To my shock and surprise, as a primary text we were using the Christian lectionary, which contains thematic descriptions of every Sunday and church observance including lesson topics, readings, liturgical colors—the proverbial "soup to nuts" and how to do it. Each student had to pick a Sunday and was assigned one church observance. I was assigned All Saints Day. It could have been worse—I realize that now—but at the time all I could think about was how a non-Christian, Unitarian Universalist was going to create, observe, and lead a group of Christian ministers through an authentic observance of their All Saints Day. After some research, which included a lot of reading, but most significantly after some deep soul-searching and reflection, I came up with what I feel was one of my better sermons.

It all started by my coming to grips with sainthood. I mean, just what did that really mean, to be a saint? Was there some way to look at saintliness outside of the church, a way that any person could appreciate? In other words, stripped of all the institutional, hierarchical, ceremonial, and liturgical language and symbolism, what did it mean to be a saint? Was this something I could really understand and feel? It was while I was asking all these questions that I found this quote in a UU church newsletter:

Becoming and being a saint does not mean being perfect but being whole; it does not mean being exceptionally
religious, or being religious at all, it means being liberated
from religiosity and religious pietism of any sort; [becoming
and being a saint] does not mean being morally better, it
means being exemplary; it does not mean being godly, but
rather being truly human; [becoming and being a saint]
does not mean being other-worldly, but it means being
deeply implicated in the practical existence of this world
without succumbing to the world or any aspect of this
world. . . . (William Stringfellow)

These then are the qualities that make for sainthood:
wholeness, liberation from religious pretentiousness, being
exemplary, being involved in living. Saintliness, then, is living out all those qualities of personhood that strive to embrace life, qualities that are always known to us yet often
remain just out of reach. Frederick Buechner puts it like this:

To be a saint is to live not with hands clenched to grasp,
to strike, to hold tight to a life that is always slipping away
the more tightly we hold it; but it is to live with the hands
stretched out both to give and to receive with gladness. To
be a saint is to work and weep for the broken and suffering
of the world, but it is also to be strangely light of heart in
the knowledge that there is something greater than the
world that mends and renews. Maybe more than anything
else, to be a saint is to know joy. Not happiness that comes
and goes with the moments that occasion it, but joy that is
always there like an underground spring no matter how
dark and terrible the night. To be a saint is to be a little out
of one's mind, which is a very good thing to be a little out of
from time to time. It is to live a life that is always giving itself away and yet is always full. (*Listening to Your Life*)

Put in these terms, it's much easier for me to talk about
saints, to talk about the people who through their wholeness, generosity of self, joy, and insanity have changed the
lives of so many, including me. And what I have discovered
as remarkable is that very few, if any, of these saints
started in unordinary ways. The saints who have shaped

my world began in the most ordinary of ways; you might even say that they were, well, they were a little crazy.

Just as the church has led many to believe that those having received sainthood have shaped the church, the holy catholic tradition, and continue shaping our world today, I would assert that each of us is surrounded by a "cloud of witnesses"—the equivalent of saints—by which our lives are led, buoyed, challenged, supported, and comforted. Despite the appearance of ordinariness, this cloud of witnesses is made unordinary because they have made us who we are today, sometimes in ways that we will never fathom. These unordinary souls include many whom we might all agree are saints, but among them are those who are not so well-known, or maybe are known only to you. Let's call them our ancestral saints. Alice Walker tells of them in this way:

> To acknowledge our ancestors means we are aware that we did not make ourselves, that the line stretches all the way back, perhaps, to God; or to Gods. We remember them because it is an easy thing to forget: that we are not the first to suffer, rebel, fight, love and die. The grace with which we embrace life, in spite of the pain, the sorrows, is always a measure of what has gone before. *(Billy Blue)*

Every time I come to church, I think of the long heritage of Unitarians and Universalists in America; I remember the mothers and fathers of my congregation's tradition who blessed us with their hard work and foresight; every time we gather on a Sunday morning, their memory and presence are evoked.

And then each one of us has family and friends-that-might-as-well-be-family that have shaped us and are shaping us still. They all comprise the unordinary souls in our lives, our saints, the cloud of witnesses who, whether we want them or not, are there. Without them we would not, we could not be who we are.

Or will be—there is a future tense to all of this. Saints and unordinary souls don't die with recognition—in fact, that's when it all begins! In recognition comes a realization, an "ah-ha!" Because now we understand—or least soon will—that you too will be a saint one day, you too will be an unordinary soul, you too will be part of someone's cloud of witnesses. In fact, it might already be happening.

Are you uncomfortable thinking of yourself in these terms? Listen to the way Maya Angelou talks about it. She was being interviewed by Cornell West at a college gathering when she said:

> Everybody here has already been paid for. And if you understand that in a part of your mind and spirit—whether the ancestors came from Ireland or Asia, Eastern Europe or South America, or from Africa, lying spoon fashion in filthy hatches of slave ships—if you understand that somebody already paid for you, and that all you have to do is prepare yourself so that you can pay for someone else who is yet to come. And act on it, act with kindness and courtesy and generosity, develop patience so that your words don't just jump out of your mouth with rudeness and you cut somebody's heart away. Take a moment. *(Restoring Hope)*

Each of our lives might feel ordinary, far from saintly. But each of us has the potential to be an unordinary soul for at least one other, if not for many—to be a saint, to be fully human, to be a witness in someone else's life.

Today, tomorrow, on any day, think of all the unordinary souls that form your cloud of witnesses, the saints in your life. And remember these words of Hannah Senesh: "There are stars whose radiance is visible on earth though they have long been extinct. There are people whose brilliance continues to light the world though they are no longer among the living."

Sanctuary

Every house of worship has a sanctuary. Of course, it may go by different names, but all congregations have a room, space, or place of enthusiasm and inspiration. A sanctuary is a safe place, a safe house; a space where we can escape from the pressures of our work-a-day routines, from sometimes harsh daily realities, and be comforted or expand our horizons or be challenged without the background noise of family traditions and politics-as-usual. A sanctuary is a breathing space, a place to catch our breath, offering us an opportunity for growing, thinking, perspective, and fellowship.

In both Christian and Jewish traditions, the words *breathe, wind, spirit,* and *life* all play off each other as if in a theological dance, something we miss out on understanding when we read only the English text. For example, like its counterparts in Hebrew and Greek, *spiritus* means "breathe." Now I never studied Greek or Latin, but I did take ancient Hebrew. And in Hebrew there's a small word that is similar. *Ruah* is the word for "wind." Often you will read in the Hebrew Scriptures about the *ruah* blowing in an area about to be holy or that is holy. *Ruah* can also be translated as "spirit." So when the spirit of God—the wind—is blowing about you, it is *ruah* in both meanings.

Just as the air we breathe is necessary to living, so too is the spirit vital to our life essence: as we must be filled with the wind in order to breathe and stay alive, so too must we be filled with the spirit of life in order to know the holy. Carolyn McDade penned the lyrics to a favorite song among Unitarian Universalists. It goes like this: "Spirit of Life, come unto me, sing in my heart all the stirrings of compassion. Blow in the wind, rise in the sea; move in the hand, giving life the shape of justice. Roots hold me close; wings set me free; Spirit of Life, come to come, come to me." With those words—words that speak about or refer to wind, air, and spirit—McDade and those who are moved by her words are in a long tradition, maybe as long as 3,000 years, of being filled with and breathing the life force of the spirit, which some have chosen to call God.

This is how we come to the word *enthusiasm* from the Greek *en-theo-ism,* literally meaning to be filled with God, as in to be filled with spirit, the spirit of the wind, of the air we breathe, the Spirit of Life. Enthusiasm then is but a spiritual version of mouth-to-mouth resuscitation—and by now I hope you begin to see the value of doing breathing exercises in the safe place called a sanctuary. It's a matter of life and death, just as breathing exercises should be and will be, always. It's a matter of enthusiasm, which is what we must bring in and leave with each time we are in our congregation's sanctuary. To be filled with the spirit, with the wind, to be filled with God—this is what we expect in our sanctuary, this has been the expectation of religious people for millennia, and this is why this safe room is so important to us. It is special, it is holy, it is a place for inspiration, it is a space for catching our breath.

Sin

Given the antiquity of the Genesis 3 story of paradise lost, humankind has been fussing over where we went wrong for a long, long time. A lot of the confusion intensified when Christians jumped onto the scene, because they significantly altered the religious landscape by changing the accepted understanding of sin. You see, for Hebrews what Adam and Eve did was not sinning so much as simply growing up—they were learning that life was not only about the comforts of paradise. The Garden story was all about *cheyt,* the Hebrew word meaning "to miss the mark," which was their definition of sin—like shooting an arrow at the target and missing. After you miss, of course it's a disappointment, but you try again, you try to hit the mark. In other words, sinning is a part of life, no different than breathing, eating, or sleeping. So we sin—what else is new! But Christians took a different slant on it—Christians went and made it personal, as if it was an affront to God. They spoke of human flaw and evil as though sin was a significant breach of the life contract that every person signed by default just by being born. Christians dogmatized sin, which reminds me of a story: An Eskimo encountered a missionary priest after morning mass and asked, "If I had not known about sin, would it have been necessary to be saved?" "Of course not," the priest told him. "Then why did you tell me?" replied the Eskimo.

Now I realize that some don't even like to hear the word *sin,* some don't agree with traditional Christian theology, while others find the word and theology simply irrelevant. Religious liberals of every kind have problems with the concept of sin. If we talk about it at all, often it comes out in such a way that no one's really sure what's being said, which is Kathleen Norris's frustration. She says: "I am a sinner, and the Presbyterian church offers me a weekly chance to come clean. . . . But the pastors can be so reluctant to use the word 'sin' that in church we end up confessing nothing except our highly developed capacity for denial. . . . It would be refreshing to answer, simply, 'I have sinned.' " (*Amazing Grace*)

Well, sin is not irrelevant for religious liberals nor is its theology misguided. Sin can still be a significant word and reality for our faith community, it's just that it needs some reframing, which is why I've always clung to the fact that the Garden story is a myth. A myth, I remind you, is based not on the facts of historical time and place, but on the facts of reoccurring themes from the human psyche. In a myth, the facts are from the story of human development. As a myth that rehearses the reoccurring themes of human denial, responsibility, and isolation, the Garden myth of Genesis 3 is as truthful a fact as World War II, troops in Kosovo, or Hurricane Floyd.

Sin then is anything that I do that isolates, ostracizes, or separates me or others from the human community (and by extension, from the web of life) which results in robbing or denying human uniqueness and potential. Call it evil or flawed behavior; call it missing the mark; call it brokeness; call it denial, repression, or reaction formation—it's all sin if it separates, ostracizes, or isolates us from the ground of our being, from that which defines us as human beings. Sin is behavior that prevents a person from living out their potential for human being-ness.

Now back to Adam and Eve, whose sin wasn't eating the fruit. It would have been a sin—a denial of their potential—if they had not eaten the fruit. No, Adam and Eve sinned—isolated and ostracized themselves—by refusing to take responsibility for what they had done.

And what does the story say they did when confronted about their disobedience? They blamed the snake! Adam and Eve's sin wasn't eating from the tree, as God had directed them not to do; it was refusing to accept responsibility for their freedom, it was in their attempt to be better, different, or above what was to become understood as humanness.

By making the reality of sin a story in perpetuating the myth of human irresponsibility and misuse of free will, early Judaism was saying that *cheyt*—missing the mark—is going to happen over and over. It's a reoccurring theme in human living. In fact, sin is a part of what it means to be human: we try to live up to our potential and we fail, we try again and we fail, over and over we try and fail. But do we stop trying? Of course not!

Now please, don't go back to work or school or tell your spouse, lover, friends, or family that I've suggested that you sin boldly or that I said that sinning is good, that the more you do it the better you'll feel, or that sin is a growth opportunity. This is not what I'm saying—well, not exactly. The truth is we do commit acts, we have thoughts that miss the mark, that are sinful: if we don't then we are not of this planet! That's what the Adam and Eve story is all about: it tells us that to be human is to fall short of expectations, to not live up to our ideals. It is a given that we will miss the mark. And yet we never quit trying to be whole, seeking oneness, completion, at-one-ment.

Spirituality

Spirituality refers to the inner dimension, a depth dimension, of every person. Every religious tradition has some facet that speaks to this spiritual side of our humanness: indigenous faiths are permeated by mysticism, Judaism has Hassidism and Kabbalah, Islam has Sufi, Christianity has numerous spiritual and mystical traditions. These, and many others, all speak to spirituality as this inner dimension of being religious.

When newcomers describe their decision to come (back) to church—not just this church, but to enter the search for a faith community—it's not uncommon to hear many say that it was the "something missing in their lives" that drove them to it. After a few more sentences, some will call this "something" spirituality—it was spirituality that was missing, though I've heard it called other names as well. Common to these sorts of descriptions has been a sense or feeling of emptiness, meaninglessness, a lack of direction, a desire for greater depth, connectedness, grounding, or rootedness.

I would estimate that tens of thousands of hungry souls go in search of finding that "something missing" every Sabbath morning. For the most part, we applaud this search, this journey. Perhaps you were once at this point in your life—perhaps you still are. The desire to satisfy our spiritual needs is important.

Yet, the change in language is telling us something. To say that so-and-so is a deeply religious person just doesn't seem to carry the same punch as saying that they are a deeply spiritual person. For example, a friend, therapist, or maybe even a minister might be actually alarmed or even uninterested and just ignore a person who expresses a desire to be more religious. But if a friend, client, or parishioner should share that they wish to be more spiritual—well, this is something! We are impressed, and heads will nod as though everyone understands exactly what this person is seeking.

Why? What's going on here? Why does *spirituality* carry more validity, integrity, interest, or energy than does *religiousness* or other words? Kathleen Norris explains:

> I wonder if we're witnessing something that, if it isn't exactly new under the sun, may be happening on an unprecedented scale: the rejection of religion itself, which tends to ground itself in communal contexts in favor of privatized spiritualities that have little context but the self. (*Hungry Mind Review*)

She may be right. It's the personal quality, the softer side, the attentive aspects of spirituality that many find appealing, whereas there's an edge to religion, a coldness that many feel is embodied by the church.

Let's look at what these words mean. *Spirituality* and its mate *soul* are still an uncomfortable fit for many. Jon Kabat-Zinn admits to just not using the words—they're too confusing, offending, or require too much work. But the words are here to stay for awhile longer. A need for spirituality, the wish for spirituality in their family life, their children's lives, these are common reasons why people come to church. So what do they mean?

Actually, like Kabat-Zinn, I too am uncomfortable with these words. The language of spirituality—to say nothing of religion and theology—is never precise, exhaustive, or final, and yet clarity is what many want. The metaphor of roots and wings is a good starting place for understanding. The soul is your roots: roots stabilize, they feed, roots provide for thirst; without roots a tree is dead. Anyone who has tried to remove roots knows that it's no easy thing. Before they had root grinders (and they aren't always 100 percent effective) not only did it take forever to get rid of roots, but even when you thought they were gone, in the spring or a year or two later up would pop a leaf or flower from the roots you thought you'd destroyed. Roots can run long, deep, and wide.

So it can be with one's soul. Soul is the core of your being, the inner light that makes you who you are; soul is your essence and identity. Some will say that it's the divine spark, a piece of the Holy, the image of God, an imprint of the sacred. Others will say that the soul is the dust, remnants, or seeds of the Universe, the Cosmos; whatever its composition, it can never be destroyed—it is immortal, eternal. Like roots, soul makes your life unique while at the same time connecting you to all that was, is, and ever will be.

And what of the spirit? Without soul, there could be no spirit. A spiritless person is one who lacks soul or is in soul trouble. Spirit is wings: your spirit soars, dips, often takes you places you didn't even want to visit. The strength of one's wings, the stamina and courage of spirit are always connected to your roots, your soul. Just how far and high and long you are willing to fly can all depend on your comfort level and endurance, and this all has to do with soul.

Spirituality is the word used to describe the interdependent workings of both spirit and soul. Spirituality is about this inner dimension, a dimension that until recently was maybe lost, discarded, unappreciated, or abused. And then, there was an awakening: the spirituality bandwagon went from a few lone travelers to a crowded convoy. But not without a reason. Maybe Diana Eck speaks for you when she writes:

> Our cultures are thirsty for whatever it is that is named with the word spirituality. Our lives are busy. Our days hurtle by with a roar. Our rooms are piled with books to read, filled with the sound of televised news reports, with minute-by-minute coverage of baseball games and national and international disasters, filled with music as we like. There

is so much to keep up with that stopping for periods of real stillness is increasingly difficult. We have practiced the routes of having, doing, going, making, getting, and keeping so frequently that we know the terrain by heart. The ways of watchfulness and attention will take both learning and unlearning. (*Encountering God*)

In order to maintain the watchfulness and attention that can heighten, deepen, or broaden spirituality, many turn to a disciplined practice. A spiritual discipline is a way of nurturing and nourishing the soul, quieting and relaxing the spirit, supporting and affirming your spirituality. James Carse mentions several ways: "Prayer, seated meditation, walking mediation, guided meditation, fasting, dancing, chanting, physical isolation, living in community, acquired poverty, self-examination, concentrated study of sacred texts, long periods of silence, guidance by a teacher, a dozen varieties of yoga, sexual excess, sexual abstinence, finding the hidden meaning of numbers, pathless wandering, devoted service to others, institutional obedience." (*Breakfast at the Victory*) All of these, and many more, are disciplined paths that some have followed with commitment and steadfastness as well as a determination and zest that would rival any twelve-hour/seven-day-a-week job, which makes you wonder just when a spiritual discipline becomes simply one more thing to do, another something to be checked from your list.

Is this the point where spirituality begins to border on narcissism and obssession? Yes, when spirituality begins to lead you in the direction of me, Me, ME! It's all about me! There's a closing down instead of an opening up to the world—or going back to my metaphor, spiritual narcissism occurs when your soul roots are growing deeper and growing wider, but it's as though your wings have been clipped, your willingness and determination to soar, explore, connect, and venture is diminishing: in spite of the soul's strength, you have limited your spirit.

So where does all of this lead? Where could it lead? While spirituality is a turning inward, an inward reading of the self through the lens of the soul and spirit, it doesn't get stuck or stay too long inside because this can result in an incredible imbalance and dishonesty. A spirituality that serves the self is narcissism. But a spirituality that serves both self and others nurtures the soul and strengthens the spirit. I really like the way Linda Underwood puts it. May this be our blessing:

All this talk of saving souls. Souls weren't made to save, like Sunday clothes that give out at the seams.

They're made for wear; they come with lifetime guarantees. Don't save your soul. Pour it out like rain on cracked, parched earth.

Give your soul away, or pass it like a candle flame. Sing it out, or laugh it up the wind.

Souls were made for hearing, breaking hearts, for puzzling dreams, remembering August flowers, forgetting hurts.

These folk who talk of saving souls! They have the look of bullies who blow out candles before you sing happy birthday, and want the world to be in alphabetical order.

I will spend my soul, playing it out like sticky string into the world, so I can catch every last thing I touch. (found in "Church of the Larger Fellowship" newsletter)

The Talents (Matthew 25)

I recall a definition of cynic and wonder how many it applies to: A cynic is not only one who "reads bitter lessons from the past, but one who is prematurely disappointed in the future." (quoted by John Buehrens in *World: Journal of the Unitarian Universalist Association*) Of course there are varying degrees of cynicism, just as there are many different kinds of dissatisfactions about virtually everything. And there's nothing wrong with being dissatisfied—there are things with which we should and must be dissatisfied.

But this isn't what I'm talking about. I'm wondering about the person who doesn't know how to or who won't or who can't say yes, the person who simply doesn't realize that yes is the answer. Yes to living, to love, to friends and family; yes to life. What does it take to really know and feel that yes is the answer?

The parable of the talents (Matt. 25:14–29) has never been a favorite of mine because at first reading it doesn't reflect a world I want anything to do with: it's got master-slave relationships, it appears to affirm a form of capitalism that is unsettling, it's about rewards and punishments that don't appear fair, and it's simply difficult to understand.

In this case, most Bibles do us a disservice by explaining that a talent is a large sum of money, and it is. But the parable is not about money—it's about talent, about gifts, it's a parable about life and saying yes to life. Look at it like this: Each of the men is given gifts with life and is told to use them as he will. Two of them take the gifts they've been given and use ("spend") them all; they invest them at a risk, a risk because living life to its fullest is always a risk for nothing is ever certain. But one of the men wants certainty. For fear that he might lose his gift, he buries his talent, refusing to use it; he's going to hide his talent and save it for a rainy day. Essentially this man is saying no to living; he will not take the risk of losing what he has. And so in the end, this man forfeits what he had because he refused to use it, which is to say, how can anyone live life without first saying yes, without the risk of having lived?

When yes is the answer, we don't want to bury our talents, we want to invest them, share them, use them up; we want to participate in living to its fullest; we seek the risk that is living and relish its opportunities. After reading and understanding the parable of the talents, it becomes clearer why the Jewish Talmud teaches a version of it which says that at death, we each will be asked to account for every permissible thing that we might have enjoyed, but didn't. Based on scriptures of this sort, Brian Swimme was led to say:

> The human is a creature that was really created for delight, for a sense of astonishment. What would our culture be like if we took this understanding as our grounding? Your purpose and worth wouldn't be the amount of commodities you have; it would be the way you could enter into the delight of life.

Who doesn't have some sense of this when things are going right—that of course we are creatures of delight and astonishment. What a great feeling to be atop our world! But it's just that, a feeling—moods will come and go. We need to embrace them all while we have them, and know that the valleys exist too. We will have both, with plenty of plateaus in between. Saying yes to life involves the peaks, valleys, and plateaus, because they all are life. How boring life would be with just one or another—I mean, how would we ever have any taste for life if every-thing tasted the same?

I marvel at the way many are capable of rising above what appear as their personal tragedies and proclaim-ing that yes is the answer. I know that we each could tell stories—some of them from our own lives—that would fill a book, a book about the human spirit, a book of talents, of people who simply would not give up on living.

One year during National Poetry Month, I was par-ticularly struck by a poem read by an African-American child. Listening to his young, passionate, and enthusias-tic voice I was moved to tears. The poem is by Langston Hughes and is entitled "Life Is Fine":

> I went down to the river. / I set down on the bank. / I tried to think but couldn't / So I jumped in and sank. / I came up once and hollered! / I came up twice and cried! / If that water hadn't a-been so cold / I might've sunk and died. / But it was / Cold in that water! / It was cold!
>
> I took the elevator / Sixteen floors above the ground. / I thought about my baby / And I thought I would jump down. / I stood there and I hollered! / I stood there and I cried! / If it hadn't a-been so high / I might've jumped and died. / But it was / High up there! / It was high!
>
> So since I'm still here livin', / I guess I will live on. / I could've died for love— / But for livin' I was born. / Though you may hear me holler, / And you may see me cry— / I'll be dogged, sweet baby, / If you gonna see me die. / Life is fine! / Fine as wine! / Life is fine!

Life is fine. With all its ups and downs, comings and goings, life can be as fine as wine. Yes is the answer. Don't bury your talents.

Tolerance

It should be no wonder that tolerance has been an enduring principle in our faith-trinity of freedom, reason, and tolerance. Time after time, intolerance has put Unitarian Universalism on a religious version of the endangered species list. Yet, now we find ourselves not only surviving, but thriving—although we have to admit that it hasn't always been due to tolerance. There are some parallels in the situation described in this story:

One Sunday morning, a minister was preaching to his congregation about tolerance of enemies. About twenty minutes into his sermon, he was getting pretty heated up and shouted out what was meant to be a series of rhetorical questions: "We've all got enemies, don't we? We've all got to learn to live with our enemies, don't we? Anybody here who doesn't have an enemy, I want you stand up right now so we can congratulate you," he shouted, knowing that no one would take him up on his offer.

But in the last row, in the corner of the sanctuary, there was one, slender, white-haired man—the elder of the church—who slowly raised his hand and started standing up. Well, the preacher was shocked. He hadn't anticipated this, but he decided he had to go with it.

"John, I understand that you don't think you have any enemies. That's wonderful, wonderful indeed."

"That's right," the old man replied. "I've got no enemies."

"Well, John, why don't you tell us how you did it. I'll bet it's tolerance, isn't it John? You tolerated those you disagreed with. That's why you get along with them all, isn't it?"

"No," John the elder replied, "it wasn't tolerance. I outlived all the SOBs!"

Well, you can't deny that John the elder is right. Outliving those who have a different view is one way of finally getting a version of tolerance. But our historical struggle—as a religious tradition and as a nation—to practice our free faith and to live side by side with those who hold other beliefs—makes clear that tolerance is usually a matter of power and not life longevity, and we're talking about political power and not what some might like to believe is civic or religious principle. It's those with power that determine the limits and boundaries of tolerance. William Schulz writes in *Finding Time:* "The powerful define the parameters of tolerance while the powerless have no choice but to abide by them." We have learned since our first days in school that ours is a nation of freedom and tolerance, where all people are treated equally and where no person is discriminated against—no matter what. Yet we know that this is not true. Tolerance has clearly been defined as to what skin colors, sexual orientations, gender, or ethnicity are deemed "appropriate."

How easily we can be rocked into the comfort of thinking that because our laws say one thing and our politicians and history books affirm it, then it must be so. Logic of this sort is a bit like the elephant who wandered onto a farm and into a chicken yard, where she began dancing a polka. The sight was not a pretty one! Crushed birds lay everywhere. At her trial, the elephant said in her defense: "Before I started, I cautioned everyone by shouting: 'Every man for himself.' "

Tolerance allows everyone to be heard—both the powerful and the less powerful, the rich and poor, majority and minority, the elephant and the chickens. Tolerance is shaped with everyone participating—not just the elite or those with power.

There's another danger that comes with the perception of tolerance, a danger that especially affects liberalism, both political and religious. This is the danger of trying to be so inclusive, embracing so many people with their dreams, ideals, and faiths, of having such a wide door and large room that once everyone is in you may not be sure why you're there. In the name of tolerance, definition has been lost.

How far in the name of inclusion—in the name of tolerance—would you be willing to go? One fall, during a presidential election, we had candidate representatives come to the church to speak. One member had lined up speakers on behalf of a perennial presidential candidate, a recognized neofascist and hate peddler. I said no. I was criticized by some who thought that my "no" wasn't very liberal, not very tolerant. The same thing happened when several falls later, members of the Maryland Ku Klux Klan wanted to come to the church and have an opportunity to state their position to the congregation: They weren't racist fear peddlers; we had been misinformed. I said, "No, thanks." Again, some members thought that wasn't very tolerant of me and didn't make the church look welcoming. The difficulty for the political and religious liberal can be summed up with this: ". . . if we set no limits at all to what is deemed tolerable, we end up in a philosophical vacuum." (Schulz)

Here then are two pitfalls of tolerance: tolerance as a tool of the powerful, a means of excluding people rather than including them; and tolerance that at its worst creates meaninglessness, that sets no limits or boundaries and thus, no definition.

Pluralism, not tolerance, is our vision. The hope for a pluralistic community is the dream I hope to make actual. I seek engagement with those who are different, who believe differently than I do. I do not seek the kind of engagement that could come with extremists who don't want meaningful engagement and dialogue, who only want a platform to spread their ideology, who don't want to be challenged with theology and ethics, who want to spread fear and hate. As a nation we tolerate such extremists because of constitutional protections that we feel keep our nation strong; but as a congregation we are obligated to make clear that we will not tolerate those who denigrate "the inherent worth and dignity of every person."

Pluralism is our vision and dream. We seek to understand those who are unlike us, we seek the challenge of meaningful engagement because we will all grow spiritually, emotionally, and intellectually. Pluralism means respecting and taking joy in our differences—not trying to melt everyone into one mold. If Unitarian Universalism is going to remain a faith that embraces, supports, and gives home to a variety of very different theological expressions, then we must talk to each other. Dialogue is the key to an effective pluralism. Just how much do you really know about the people living around you? Are you willing to risk the challenge that might come with finding out more about them? Are you willing to risk having to verbalize what it is you believe and why you are a Unitarian Universalist? Dialogue with each other is what it is all about.

If we won't talk with each other, then pluralism doesn't stand a chance and an inconsequential and meaningless tolerance will prevail. If we will talk with each other, if we will share the diversity that makes our congregations rare and outstanding, then not only can we learn from and take joy in our differences, but we can share our diversity and the reality that beyond this diversity we are sisters and brothers in one unique family.

Unitarian Universalism

Several years ago, at a conference that some of us attended, one of the speakers challenged us by saying that we must be able to share our religion in one sentence—that's all we get because that's all a person will listen to. If you can't do it in one sentence, you've lost them. This makes it very difficult for Unitarian Universalists, who have been accused of never speaking in sentences, but in paragraphs! That one sentence doesn't have to explain everything; it's probably better if it doesn't. But it must give a person some sense of what it is you believe. And it must use words that your listener understands as religious, which is to say that if you are describing your religion, then you've got to use the language of religion—not physics or philosophy, not sociology, anthropology or psychology, not politics, ethics, humanism, or paganism. I know that these are all important for many of us and may have contributed significantly to shaping our religious beliefs, but they must come later and not in a one-sentence description of our religion.

This sentence must sound "religious" to the listener, it must maintain the integrity of our heritage, and it must leave the listener wanting to know more—which is your opportunity to then speak in paragraphs! With all of this in mind, for some time I have flirted with a one-sentence definition of our religion. This is it:

Ours is a religion whose theology is unitarian, its faith universalist, its worship creedless, its polity congregational.

Theology, faith, worship, and polity: it's these that shape
a religious tradition, it's these that people wish to know
about when they ask, "What is your religion?"

Our theology is unitarian. There have always been
unitarians—they're as old as religion. Unitarianism is
simply a statement about the oneness of God and the unity
of experience. With the birth of Christianity, though, trinitarianism was eventually hatched: a Godhead of Father,
Son, and Holy Spirit, three yet one. Trinitarians and unitarians debated the merits of these doctrines for three centuries before it was finally declared that the Holy Trinity
was the official position of Christendom, while the unitarians were told to shut up or deal with the consequences.
Well, for centuries after, unitarians didn't shut up and dealt
with the very harsh results, which often included death.

There have always been heretics, the religious liberals, who chose to believe in the unity of God, the irre-
ducible character of the Eternal, the oneness of the
Transcendent, the whole and complete nature of Life, the
intradependency of the Cosmos. Anything less than this
is a travesty, a mockery, a sham; it closes one's senses to
the realities that we know are true.

Today, regardless of what particular form of unitarian
belief some may choose, holding a unitarian theology
means this:

It means acknowledging and respecting the interdependent web of all living things. The world, life, the
Cosmos—what some would call God—is one, a Unity. To
reduce it, to remove any one piece from the whole, to chop
it up into smaller pieces, is to weaken it, to change its basic nature. It means celebrating one's whole self, even in
matters of religion: the use of reason and critical study in
all matters of belief is understood and encouraged. Unitarian theology is not merely a leap of faith, but a leap
guided by wisdom.

Unitarianism means respect and tolerance for all
people, for the whole of creation.

While theology is the study of and reflection on faith,
faith is what we use to get through the day, it's our ongoing

beliefs, the ground of our being, it's what helps us make sense of what is not always a world or life that lends itself to sense. It's our faith that gets us through the night. Many (and maybe most) who have come to this religion have done so through the door (and name) of unitarianism—it's a theology that many find initially appealing. But once we are here, we discover that we are in fact universalists. Unitarianism has always been the brains of our movement, but universalism has always been its heart and soul.

Just as the unitarians had debated with the trinitarians during the early centuries of the Common Era, universalists also took on those who claimed that God was punishing and vindictive by nature, separating humankind into those saved from hell and those condemned to the eternal fires. The universalists preached that God was loving and held out to all the promise of salvation: universal forgiveness and atonement would be given to all, not just the elect.

Eventually, most of Christendom would back off its threat of eternal damnation at the hands of a vengeful, wrathful God—they saw the appeal of the supportive and nurturing message of universal salvation, a message that by the turn of the century had made Universalism one of the largest denominations in North America.

Today, the fear of burning in hell isn't what it used to be, but the faith of universalism persists.

Universalism says that love is at the basis of all relationships: love between us, between each person and their God. Love is at the heart of the religious experience.

Universalism says that this message of love and salvation can be shared by every person no matter who they are and that this is such good news that it is incumbent on us to share it every opportunity we get.

Universalism proclaims that the world, our universe, the Cosmos, God is receptive to our needs, welcoming to our presence—we are meant to be here. So trust, be open, be responsive. These postures and attitudes are critical to our way of living.

Our unitarian theology and our universalist faith are integral to our Sunday morning worship, which remains creedless. We have no statements of religious belief—no dogma—that are repeated in unison every week when we gather. Our religion and worship are creedless for three reasons.

First, creedal religion suggests that humankind's spiritual and religious growth have reached a conclusion. Creeds, rather than encouraging more searching, growing, and knowing, freeze and stop one's pilgrimage, eliminating the process, affirmation, and celebration of new insights (what has been referred to as continuous revelation). Creedal worship is akin to saying, "Here's the answer—just say this."

Second, ours is a creedless religion and worship since it is something other than creeds that bind us together. Time after time when I have asked Unitarian Universalists what keeps them going to church, a major reason is the community, fellowship, each other—it's covenant, the commitments and promises that we voluntarily make to each other. It's the relationships with others, not creeds, that bind us together as a congregation.

Finally, we place the highest value on the free mind, which means the freedom of religious belief. For centuries, freethinking religious liberals have been ostracized, castigated, and put in harm's way because they wouldn't relinquish their free mind to the majority view. And so, to protect, celebrate, support, and nurture the free mind and the freedom of religious belief, ours remains a creedless religion. On Sunday mornings you will not find or hear unison statements of belief that all are expected to recite and affirm.

Unitarian in theology, universalist in faith, creedless in worship—when you understand all of these it makes sense that the way we organize ourselves is with congregational polity. Polity is governance, and congregational polity "sees no power that extends beyond those who elected them, that is, a congregation . . . which has the right and responsibility to choose and ordain its own clergy, elect its own officers, direct them in the course of their duties, and replace them when necessary . . . there are no synods, bishops, or other persons empowered elsewhere with authority over a congregation." (*Interdependence: Renewing Congregational Polity*)

Baptists, Disciples of Christ, United Church of Christ, Quakers, and Jews all organize themselves according to congregational polity, but none of them are quite as radical in their form of governance as we are. Just as our nation was built on the tradition of the town meeting, our heritage is built on the pillars of congregational polity. Every member of the congregation has a voice in what goes on, every member has the opportunity to participate, vote, support, and determine the future of this church.

So, there you have it: polity, worship, faith, and theology. If you haven't already, perhaps soon you will find yourself in a similar situation as did one minister:

Seated between strangers at a dinner party and caught off guard, he lets the cat slip out.

"You are a what?"

"A Unitarian Universalist."

"Oh, I see," the man says, but obviously he doesn't. He is rescued by the woman to his right.

"I've never really understood just what it is you Unitarians believe. You are Christians, aren't you?"

"Not exactly. I mean, we were and some of us still are but most of us are not."

"You don't believe in Jesus?"

"Not in an orthodox way, certainly. Many of us value his teaching but few, if any of us, believe that he was resurrected on the third day or that he was God."

"What about immortality?"

"Well, I guess you'd have to say that we're pretty much divided on that one."

"But at least you all believe in God?" interrupts the man across the table.

"Not exactly. Many of us do, if each in his or her own way. Others of us do not find the concept of God a useful one."

"What then do you believe?" the bewildered hostess politely asks. (adapted from F. Forrester Church)

So how will you answer? Go ahead and try it. One sentence, seventeen words:

Ours is a religion whose theology is unitarian, its faith universalist, its worship creedless, its polity congregational.

I'll guarantee you this: the silence that follows will give you plenty of time to plan your next move!

Welcoming Congregation

As Unitarians our theology has historically affirmed the interdependency of life. We embrace life as a whole, as a unity—we don't reduce it to parts, pieces needing elaborate explanations and dogma to keep them from falling even further apart. As Unitarians we have a theology that celebrates the wholeness of life. As Universalists, we embrace a faith stance that accepts all people as children of God—all people are part of the whole: Universalist theology announces that there are no unsaved or unaccepted, no rejected or cast out. Our Universalist heritage shares the good news that all people—all living things—have a place at the table of life, that everyone has a chair with their name on it.

Now oddly enough, our messages of unity and acceptance have never been well-received. From the early centuries after the death of Jesus, when theological unitarians and universalists were on the losing end of debates, to the formalization of our institutional church life in Europe and the United States, right down to the present day, Unitarian Universalists have always been on the outside looking in. You might say that our entire history has been one of being unwelcome.

We know how it feels to be unwelcome: historically we have been on the edges, have walked the boundaries, have been pushed to the outer rim, have had no place at the table. Because of this past of unwelcome-ness, we often go out of our way to be welcoming: our theology, our history, and our polity all demand that we celebrate the interdependent web of life by affirming and promoting the inherent worth and dignity of every person, seeking justice, equity, and compassion by acceptance of one another.

So why, some wonder, isn't it enough to simply say that all people are welcome? Why do we need to designate ourselves as a Welcoming Congregation? Why must we single out gays, lesbians, bisexuals, and transgendered persons? Isn't it enough to say we are open and accepting to all?

No, it's not enough—for at least three reasons. It's not enough to say that all people are welcome because our nation, our cities and communities, the faith congregations that people attend, all have long histories of saying that all people are welcome. But as we know, too often these have been just words. For example, our nation's Constitution has reminded us for centuries that all people are created equal and are endowed with rights to life, liberty, and the pursuit of happiness—but we know from history and experience that these were often empty words. There have always been those who are closed out from and not protected by the Constitution. So, in order to remedy this, we have had to name, we have had to single out, we have had to target particular groups who needed protection, who needed to be welcome because their rights weren't guaranteed as we had thought, as we had assumed—they were not invited to the welcome table as the invitation said.

It has never been good enough just to say that we accept all people equally, because there are always some who are "more accepted" than others; our histories are filled with those who have been left behind and ignored because they weren't part of the accepted group. Understand this too: I don't like the politics that comes with special designations. Yet I don't believe for a second that people of color or women or people with handicaps or disabilities could have nearly the promises and hopes they have today had consciousness not been raised and changes made. Why do we think it will be any different when it comes to sexual orientation?

It's not good enough to just say all people are ᶐ
all are welcome. We know that all haven't ᐸ
aren't—and a big step is taken when this is naᵐᵉᵘ ᵖᵉ-
cause there is power in naming. When we name something, it becomes visible, it's no longer hidden, it enters
into our reality. Our histories are full of secrets that are
barriers to emotional and spiritual growth—obstacles to
wholeness and acceptance, at the national, community,
and personal levels. And there is power in naming, naming the hidden. By designating ourselves as a Welcoming
Congregation, we are naming, and in that act we are empowering and liberating our gay, lesbian, and bisexual
brothers and sisters to come here as they are; we are empowering and liberating every member of our congregation to model for their children and their neighbors what
it means to be accepting and welcoming; we are empowering and liberating the Unitarian Universalist liberal
gospel that proclaims and celebrates that we are one. We
must name this issue, for in naming we are empowering
and liberating our heritage of wholeness and acceptance.

It's not good enough to just say all are welcome. We
must be intentional, we must name, we must be direct, because being part of a faith community (being part of any
religious community) means meeting head-on those issues and obstacles that stand in the way of our at-one-
ment. To be whole, to be at peace with ourselves, to be at
one with life means not just celebrating all that's good and
great about life, but also wrestling with our fears, those
things which we would probably prefer not to name. Issues of sexual orientation go to the very heart of our being,
to our essence, to our identity—all of which have profound
and far-reaching religious and spiritual implications. I
can't imagine why this discussion *wouldn't* prompt feelings of fear (doubt, anxiety, anger, disgust, or avoidance).
To begin raising questions of sexual orientation is going to
issues at the heart of who and what we are, affirming or
questioning assumptions we have made all our lives.

And this is where it's supposed to happen! This is
church—we are a community of faith. This is where we're

supposed to be examining and promoting what afflicts the comfortable and comforts the afflicted. This is where we speak truth to power in love. Yes, it can be scary. Yes, it is often uncertain. Yes, naming the secrets can hurt. And it can be empowering, liberating, affirming, and nurturing. Church is where it's at!

Naming ourselves as a Welcoming Congregation—as a congregation that is intentionally inclusive and expressive of the presence, gifts, and particularities of gay, lesbian, and bisexual persons—affirms and promotes the promise and vision as boldly set forth in our Unitarian Universalist Principles and Purposes. There is no room for anything other than this. It is a matter of faith integrity.

There are three steps required of integrity, or deciding right from wrong. First is discernment: discussing, holding meetings, and planning. We have to educate and inform ourselves.

Second is acting. After planning and researching comes working with the leadership of the church to see that every person has had multiple opportunities to participate. This process must be informative, inclusive, and open.

After discernment and acting, the final step of integrity is going public—letting others know of our decision and what we are going to do about it. Going public is critical to integrity; some argue that without it you fall short because then your faith is kept a secret and there's no accountability, then you're left with cheap integrity.

Faith integrity is so important. You see, there are not a lot of opportunities that we have for the bold, public, institutional affirmation of our faith. In this sense, I have heard Unitarian Universalism described as a seamless faith—we leave no traces of our religion. This has prompted some to ask, which I ask of you: If you were arrested and brought to trial for being a Unitarian Universalist, would there be enough evidence to convict you? Which is also to wonder: Does anybody know? Does anybody care?

One summer I performed a service of union for two women. When it came to the exchange of vows, the father of one of the women burst into tears, sobbing and trembling to the end of the service. I never talked with him afterwards. But several months later, I received a letter from him. He thanked me for performing the service. It was a very honest, confessional letter in which he spoke of how difficult it had been for his wife and him—especially for him—but they loved their daughter no matter what, and they love her partner. He concluded with these words:

> You probably couldn't help but notice my crying—I'm sorry if I distracted you. It suddenly struck me as I heard my daughter speak about her love for her partner, it hit me how ironic and sad it was. We live in a world of hate, loneliness and fear. And there was my daughter and her partner, madly in love with each other—and they will spend much of their lives having to hide their love, not allowed to share it with others.
>
> It will be difficult for them, I know. A positive side to all this is not only are they each with the love of their life, but that we learned there are people like you and places like your church where they will be free, where they don't have to hide who they are. Thank you and God bless the Unitarians.

It's at times like this, with letters like this, that I'm thankful that I've left behind enough evidence that would convict me of my faith, of my Unitarian Universalism. Affirming and promoting the inherent worth and dignity of every person; justice, equity, and compassion in human relations; acceptance of one another—that's what being a Welcoming Congregation means. It means living our Principles. We can accept nothing less.